Reptiles in Love

Don Ferguson, Ph.D.

Reptiles in Love

Ending Destructive Fights
and Evolving Toward
More Loving Relationships

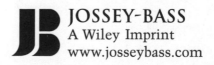
JOSSEY-BASS
A Wiley Imprint
www.josseybass.com

Published by Jossey-Bass
A Wiley Imprint
989 Market Street, San Francisco, CA 94103-1741   www.josseybass.com

Jossey-Bass books and products are available through most bookstores. To contact Jossey-
Bass directly call our Customer Care Department within the U.S. at 800-956-7739, outside
the U.S. at 317-572-3986, or fax 317-572-4002.

Jossey-Bass also publishes its books in a variety of electronic formats. Some content that
appears in print may not be available in electronic books.

Library of Congress Cataloging-in-Publication Data

Ferguson, Don, date.
   Reptiles in love : ending destructive fights and evolving toward more loving
relationships / Don Ferguson.— 1st ed.
        p. cm.
   Includes bibliographical references and index.
   ISBN-13: 978-0-7879-8320-8 (cloth)
   ISBN-10: 0-7879-8320-9 (cloth)
   1. Man-woman relationships.   2. Couples—Psychology.   I. Title.
HQ801.F468 2006
646.7'8—dc22   2005030771

Printed in the United States of America
FIRST EDITION
HB Printing   10 9 8 7 6 5 4 3 2 1

Contents

Preface

Be Like Elvis! But Less Dead

Some time ago I heard a program on National Public Radio in which they were describing Elvis Presley's first attempted recording. It was in 1954 at Sun Studios, for Sam Phillips. At that time crooners were immensely popular, and Elvis was trying to croon a slow, melancholy love song, a skill that we well know he possessed. This first time in a studio, however, he just couldn't get it right. They played one of his takes, and he sounded tense and uncomfortable, a young man trying too hard. As the story goes, the evening wore on with repeated failures. Elvis became frustrated, and the other musicians were tired and ready to go home. When he gave up on the song and began to just play for fun, he sang a fast rock song, "That's Alright, Mama." Singing for his own amusement and unaware that Phillips was still recording, Elvis tore into that song with a vengeance. In this recording you hear the power and energy that made him the King.

This story struck me as a parallel to what I want to tell you in this book. To me, the moral of the Elvis story is that when you relax and let your full creative juices flow, you'll be at your best. Everything will come out better, and you'll reach creative heights that you were never aware you could manage. When you and your partner can slow things down, approach each other in a calm and confident manner, and employ the best of your creativity and artfulness, wonderful things can happen.

Depending on which statistic you look at, divorce rates in America run at about 50 percent of marriages. There is a reported slight decline of late, and one hopes that this trend will continue. Divorce rates are used as a common marker of unsuccessful relationships—but they don't tell the most critical story. We'll talk about divorce later in this book, but for now, consider a more routine relationship tragedy. Think for a moment of the people who won't be touched by an affectionate partner today. The statistics on domestic violence are horrifying, yet think of those who dread going home tonight, not necessarily in fear of violence but simply because of the tension and anger they're likely to experience. Think of those who won't be offered a kind or supportive word and will likely offer none in return.

Often, as my wife and I cuddle or simply sit and talk, I think about the countless people who rarely experience that kind of comfort and reassurance. What causes people who were once in love to lose sight of each other and drift into emotional distance or open animosity? This is the primary question. By the time we focus on causes of divorce, it's far too late. We must first understand the basic needs that drive partners apart and that substitute distance and fear for affection and admiration.

In the following chapters, I hope to present a clear understanding of why couples lash out against one another, and a reasonable approach to getting these self-destructive and relationship-destroying processes under control.

Acknowledgments

I am lucky. I have been surrounded by geniuses and artists in caring. First and above all I must thank my wife, Gabriele, for her love, support, and loyalty. Because I don't write poetry, I offer her this little book. Together we have discovered the wild romanticism of a close and loving partnership. She has always been there for me, and her beauty, intelligence, humor, and unstinting love continue to surprise me after all these years. In addition to all her other talents, she has painstakingly read and edited every word of this manuscript. She is the one.

I also want to thank my son, Patrick, who reminds me that I am not as smart as I may think I am. Patrick's humor and energy push me to try to stay a little young. From the day he was born, Patrick has reeducated me about love.

This is also in memory of my parents, Claude and Lorena Ferguson, and of my wife's parents, Rudolf and Frieda Thaler, to whom we owe a great deal. Also in fond memory of Dr. Stuart Frager, a brilliant and humorous mentor who helped me so much early in my career and first inspired and guided my interest in family systems.

This book arose from collaborations with my talented friends and colleagues, the intelligent and caring people of Dean Health Systems, in Madison, Wisconsin. I want to express my heartfelt gratitude to the courageous and dedicated Dean staff and to the patients who entrust themselves to us.

Specifically, this book would not have been possible without the support and consultation of my friend and colleague Denise Beckfield. Peter Clagnaz has provided friendship, support, and guidance and has dramatically affected my life and career. Peter always makes me want to be a little smarter. Barbara Brigham has been a tremendous friend, colleague, mentor, group co-therapist and co-presenter. I have greatly appreciated her in all these roles; further, she read and commented on early drafts of chapters for this book. That took courage.

Amazing friends and colleagues, such as Michael Bernhard, Joe Cousin, Tom Crabb, Julia Hay, Emily Hauck, Janet Swain, and Linda Wilhelmi, continue to inspire me and shape my work. Thanks also to Kent Peterson, who lent a great deal of support in the development of my seminars and this book. I also want to thank Ann Smith, Sue Phillips, Deb Hensel, Denise Sunderlage, and Carol Pipino, the unsung heroes, for their incredible support, skills, and intelligence over many years of clinical practice. I particularly wish to thank the couples therapists who have significantly affected my work: Bill Cohn, Donna

Defoe, Avis Elson, Nancy Getz, Ann Herrold-Peterson, Raymond Koziol, and Lynn Silverman. This is not to slight the rest of the team. All are skilled and talented professionals and I cannot imagine a better group of people. We have studied, lectured, consulted, grieved, and laughed together. I can't express what it has meant to work with this committed, ethical, and profoundly intelligent group of people.

Special mention must go to the people directly responsible for the process of publishing this book. My agent, Gary Heidt of the Imprint Literary Agency, has put up with a lot from me and has really come through in preparing this book for the market. Alan Rinzler at Jossey-Bass has been creative and inspiring in guiding me through the restructuring of this book and has finessed this book into what I believe is now a very useful guide. But I save the best for last. Sharyn Kolberg rewrote my original drafts and transformed a lot of information into a cohesive and readable manuscript. I have greatly admired her patience and her ability to accomplish massive restructuring and rewrites and still retain my ideas and language.

Of course, the real learning occurs in actually doing therapy. I do want to express special thanks to the many individuals and couples who have allowed me to experience some portion of their personal stories. It is an immense step of faith to see a therapist, and particularly challenging to see a marriage therapist. I very much appreciate your courage and your willingness to educate me about relationships.

Don Ferguson
Blanchardville, Wisconsin

Reptiles in Love

This book is dedicated to my son, Patrick,
who probably can't imagine how important he is to me.

Introduction

"Doctor," the patient said, raising and lowering
his left shoulder several times, "it hurts when
I do this."
"Well, for heaven's sake," replied the helpful
physician. "Stop doing that!"

There is a lot of good advice available on how to solve couples issues. The hard part is taking that advice. Often couples try to change things for the better, only to fail repeatedly. With each failure they feel more helpless and betrayed, reducing their chances for an improved relationship. As in the old joke here, couples receive advice on how to improve their communication and stop injuring each other; what clinicians and writers fail to explain is why troubled but well-intentioned couples sometimes just can't *stop doing that*. When two caring and essentially good people simply cannot stop hurting each other, what's wrong—and what are they supposed to do?

Are you sometimes stunned at the sight of a once happy couple dissolving into bitter rage or quiet despair? Do you wonder why so many attempts at improving relationships end poorly? Or why so many partners commit embarrassing and harmful acts against one another? Are you puzzled by how often love turns to injury and anger? It turns out that the answers to these questions are found in the basic biology of human beings and their *normal* reactions to being threatened.

All human beings have what is called the *fight-or-flight* response. It is ruled by the primitive part of the brain, which is composed of the brain stem, and the limbic system including the amygdala—those areas of the brain that control emotional responses as well as such functions as eating, sleeping, sexual arousal, fighting, and running away from danger. This is what I will be calling the Reptilian Brain. It is not creative, it cannot learn complex data, and it is unable to consider the consequences of its actions. A person who is stressed or threatened will respond in a reptilian fashion and will attempt either to defeat or escape from the perceived threat. The reptile doesn't soothe; it either kills and eats, or runs away.

When our relationships are not as picture-perfect as we would like them to be, when we are threatened in any way—by internal or external forces—we react instinctively with the Reptilian Brain. That's why this book is called *Reptiles in Love,* and my purpose is to help couples in trouble move their responses up the evolutionary ladder to more rational, creative, and loving interactions.

This book is not a treatise on how to have a perfect relationship. I'm not trying to tell you how to live, or to intrude on the good things that you and your partner may already have together. The special and diverse qualities of relationships should at all times be respected. I've worked with couples for many years, but I would never claim to understand all that occurs between two people—because the truth is that we're not easily understood, analyzed, or explained. Relationships are complex blends of events, genetics, cultures, histories, and needs. No relationship is exactly like any other relationship; each one is unique and presents its own joys, strengths, and challenges.

But what all relationships have in common is that they happen between human beings, all of whom come with the same standard equipment: bodies, brains, and emotions. In all kinds of unions, including marriages, heterosexual and gay relationships, parent-child bonds, and business relationships, primary physical processes (like the fight-or-flight reflex) exist that affect all interactions. Beginning then at a place where there is commonality—our bodies—makes sense, and understanding normal human interactions under conditions of challenge or stress is the most useful starting point.

The Business of Romance

Many couples fail in their attempts to improve their relationship because they place too much pressure on themselves. They try to speak differently with their partner, yell less, be more polite or more helpful, or enter therapy. Their aim is to recapture the romance they once had. In my seminars I explain that I do not take a romantic approach to my work. "But," you might say, "you're working with intimate partners. How can you *not* take a romantic approach?" I'm glad you asked. Some therapists, encouraging couples' romantic aims, push for increased intimacy too quickly. If you and your partner have experienced defeats in your relationship, you'll need to remove various obstacles (which will be discussed later) before you feel sufficiently safe to become intimate. Attempting too early to gaze into each other's eyes or spend too much time together will only increase the tension between the two of you.

When I work with a couple, my first goal is to reduce the intensity and fear that keeps the couple separated, distant, or angry. I take a rather businesslike approach so that we can work toward partnership— a businesslike relationship emphasizing trust and safety. If the individuals can develop enough trust between them to act as good partners, then they can move on to friendship. If they begin to relax and enjoy each other as friends, they will move forward, once again, to intimacy. Such an approach may seem like a slow process, but it isn't. With reduced tension and threat, partners quickly become more creative and playful with each other. When partners are functioning at their best, they can not merely tolerate but also respect and celebrate each other's individual differences. This acceptance of each other is critical to building intimacy.

What the Hell Happened to Us?
The Death of Humor and Joy

You've probably already noticed that as stress and tension increase, your ability to stand back and look at your situation humorously deteriorates. A witty comment or joke, which might have made your partner laugh when you first met, is now met with only an icy stare. This time your partner hears the joke as an attack or as a show of disdain. Did you mean it that way or was your partner stressed and prepared to hear the worst possible meaning? Or is it possible that in the midst of your own stress, your attempt at humor did indeed have a trace of bitterness and threat in it?

For most of us, humor performs a necessary service to our health and well-being. The role of humor in health is well documented. Humor places a boundary around difficult things so that they become more manageable. Humor lightens heavy feelings and thoughts that might otherwise be perceived as frightening and overwhelming. This may be why many of us are driven to joke about terrible things.

Early in their relationship, two individuals become intoxicated by one another, just as surely as by alcohol or marijuana. They find delight, humor, and endearment in almost everything they experience together. They can laugh over minor disagreements. They may experience worry and tension over whether they are truly loved enough, but they haven't yet experienced injury and betrayal. Without such injury, their bodies do not go on full alert in response to minor disagreements or threats. They're not yet paranoid. Life is, well, good.

And Now, on a Personal Note . . .

When people come to see me for couples therapy, they're in for a lot of hard work. But we also usually laugh together. I love comedy. My office, in a medical center, is the size of a standard examining room. My walls are crowded with "professional wallpaper": the certificates that suggest that the University of Kansas, the State of Wisconsin, and other organizations approve of me as a psychologist. There is also a selection of pictures of old-time comedians like Laurel and Hardy, Charlie Chaplin, and the Three Stooges—comic masters who will always have a place in my practice. I watch for humor taking place between my patients, and when bitterness and sarcasm move toward warm, shared amusement, I rejoice.

Later on in the book, I'll be describing such things as the physical process by which partners anticipate injury and prepare to defend themselves, often self-destructively. This is serious stuff. That's why I have interspersed jokes throughout the book—as a means of bringing your brain to a playful position, which is its highest level of functioning for personal communication. I hope you recognize many of the old jokes, because to me, old jokes are like old friends. The recognition and security of knowing them is part of the fun.

Humor should also shake things up a bit. Some of the best comedy works because it takes something you think you understand well in a direction that you never would have expected. This breaks up the primitive thinking patterns described throughout the book. Obviously, humor doesn't work for everyone, nor for anyone all the time, but if you find yourself chuckling now and again as you go through this difficult process, I've done a large part of my job.

Case studies appear throughout the book as well. I've tried to show them in a slightly exaggerated, amusing, yet instructive light. They're meant to be entertaining but also to show common relationship behaviors, some probably familiar. You may recognize your own behavior in them. None of the case studies is an exact description of any couple I have treated; they're only snapshots of behaviors I've seen during treatment. More exact descriptions of specific couples would not be fair.

How the Book Works

This book is divided into three parts. Part One, "Understanding the Reptile in Us," builds a case for how and why couples push each other away. This section describes the origins and development of relationship problems, as well as the need for safety in approaching changes or increased intimacy. We'll also explore specific relationship problems and difficulties in renewing your connection. You will already be gathering hints on how to recognize and lessen the impact of negative behaviors.

Part Two, "Five Steps to Ending Destructive Fights and Evolving Toward More Loving Relationships," provides specific recommendations for changing negative patterns of behavior and practicing higher-level interactions with one another. The five steps begin with slowing everything down and evaluating yourself and your relationship, and then developing more organized approaches to needs and problems. As you progress through this discussion, from developing partnership skills through building intimacy, you will be applying some general rules to a variety of special circumstances.

The steps are presented to you as guidelines, as positive suggestions that you and your partner may find helpful when you're trying to sort things out. The two of you will want to cycle through these steps and select the practices that are most useful to your relationship.

As you and your partner attempt to implement this process, however, one or both of you may experience some discomfort. It may be that some component of the behavior feels embarrassing, or you simply are not ready for it. Does that mean that you've failed? Absolutely not!

Everything you do in working on your relationship is merely an experiment. I will say this again later, so you don't have to write it down yet. The point is extremely important, however. If you don't achieve what you consider acceptable improvement in your relationship after completing the three, four, or five steps, it doesn't mean that your relationship is doomed or that your partner doesn't care enough. It means that the particular process you tried was not right for you at this time, and it's time for a new experiment!

Part Three, "Special Issues for Evolving Reptiles," examines betrayal, couples therapy, and divorce through the understanding of the Reptilian Brain and the methods described in Part Two. Keep the book handy. You may wish to go back and look at specific applications, particularly from Part Two. Finally, there is a Resources section at the end of this book that provides guidance to excellent references in specific areas of concern.

––––––––––––

Reptiles in Love is about normal human functioning under stress. If partners in a relationship can understand their most basic physical reactions to each other, they can also learn ways to manage challenges to intimacy more effectively. If you begin this process by thinking that you'll find out what's wrong with your partner, then this is not the book for you. To improve a relationship, you must be willing to examine closely your own behavior, emotions, traditions, and methods of defending yourself. All couples therapy is also individual therapy. If you're willing to look at what you bring to the relationship, then we can work together effectively. If you're willing to reexamine yourself, your partner, and the reasons you're with him or her, you'll be able to relax and have some fun. I'm not trying to direct your relationship or convince you to stay with your partner, even though there is strong evidence that vital and lasting relationships are good for people. Although some of the reasons partners fight and leave each other are lame at best, no one can tell anyone else how to live.

Lowering Intensity and Healing

Establishing safety is serious business and needs to be the first consideration in beginning to improve your relationship. Your initial goal is not to solve problems but to reduce tension and pain. As you work through this book, and practice reducing tension and soothing one another, follow the points listed here. You will then be able to reestablish a sense of safety and cooperation and to move on toward reigniting intimacy.

- Understand the biological nature of stress and anxiety.

- Recognize that most of what you argue about is just business, and all business is negotiable.

- Recognize the patterns in which you and your partner raise each other's anxiety and anger.

- Encourage your brain to use organizational and reasoning skills to clarify your needs.

- Examine what you most need in moments of stress and anxiety and ask for help from your partner.

- Develop structures, rules, and methods for soothing each other when exhausted, angry, or anxious.

- Recognize that your partner's anxiety is not necessarily about you being bad, stupid, or incompetent; doing so will allow you to settle down and be helpful, even *playful*.

Playfulness is an important form of intimacy. When you can enjoy humor and creativity with your partner, you will most likely feel closer. Working on your relationship should be an adventure, and this book is an invitation to explore yourself and each other. If you discover new information about one another and new skills for interacting in a cooperative and loving fashion, then you are well advised to work on redeveloping your intimacy. Your new skills will lay the groundwork for exploring a deeper connection between you.

Finally, I should mention that the description of the Reptilian Brain in this book is admittedly oversimplified. The sympathetic and parasympathetic nervous systems and many other aspects of the human body influence our emotional reactions. I've included some additional references in the Resources section for those interested in greater detail on this physiological marvel. The metaphor of the Reptilian Brain is, however, an easy way to remind ourselves of what's really happening when we feel hurt, angry, fearful, or overwhelmed—and that we can, by deliberately reverting to our higher-level, rational brain functions, reconnect as communicating, caring, human couples.

Part I

Understanding the Reptile in Us

1

The Dinosaur Legacy
Why We Fight Poorly

War is the unfolding of miscalculations.
Barbara Tuchman, The Guns of August (1962)

Couples fight. It's been that way for as long as humankind has been on earth. Some couples fight and make up, fight and make up, and still have healthy, stable relationships. No harm, no foul. For other couples, the fighting causes such deep and abiding psychic pain that they've got no choice but to uncouple themselves. Still others remain in tension-filled, angry, and distant relationships with little access to affection or comfort.

Here's what most people don't understand: fighting is natural. Fighting is also quite normal. It comes from the deepest, most primitive, most "reptilian" part of our brains, and, as we shall see throughout this book, this oldest remnant of our evolutionary development can undermine the most reasonable, "human" parts of ourselves to cause horrific damage and destruction.

The upside of this is that once we understand where the fighting instinct originates and just why it is that we fight so poorly, we can do something about it. We can stop being petty, mean, and cruel to those we care about. We can stop interpreting our partner's words and gestures as personal affronts. We can evolve from irrational, hurtful combatants and form healthy and satisfying relationships.

REPTILES IN LOVE

Ozzie and Harriet Don't Live Here Anymore

Peter and Janet have been married for eight years. They have two children, good jobs, and many common interests. Their friends see them as "the perfect couple." Behind closed doors, however, the story is quite different. They often find themselves in the middle of the most ridiculous arguments, unable to stop before hurting each other.

They argue over the usual big three—money, kids, and sex—but they also argue over whether one of them shut a cabinet door extra hard or was sufficiently careful with the groceries. They fight bitterly over television shows and whether one of them goes to sleep too late at night. They circle and stalk each other like guerrilla fighters, waiting for the next insult or attack. An outsider would note the critical, angry jabs that each delivers and the genuine surprise of the attacker when he or she is counterattacked or abandoned. The couple hide this from their friends and family, and only their closest confidants know that they are having any trouble.

They tell themselves they're keeping this animosity a secret from their kids, but we all know that's impossible. Children pick up emotional storm warnings with an accuracy that would put any Doppler system to shame. Peter and Janet slowly begin to realize that their children have been demonstrating significant symptoms of stress all along (sleep problems, stomachaches, temper tantrums, and increased difficulties at school).

By the time Peter and Janet decided to seek help, Janet was threatening divorce. It's not a huge revelation that we often treat those closest to us as though they were our enemies. It's incredibly painful to realize that someone you love—and who you thought loved you—can suddenly call you the worst names, insult you or your family, ignore your needs, or even physically harm you. We enter relationships with excitement, physical arousal, and romantic views of our lover's perfection and unique love for us. Inevitably, we feel betrayed. That's just the way it is. It's impossible to sustain an unrealistic attraction to each other, one based on the concept of an idealized, romantic, uplifting, and beautifully perfect union.

Actually, this is the good news. We are not robots, nor are we angels. We possess faults, sins, and odd beliefs, all of which make us interesting to one another. The bad news is that the very traits we often initially identify as most attractive in our partners, or that seem critical to the partnership, can also become the traits we most vehemently resent.

When Peter and Janet met, they were both a couple of years out of painful breakups with prior lovers. They were amazed at the instant connectedness they felt toward one another. Peter was working two jobs at the time and was struggling to recoup from huge debts he had incurred trying to keep his former lover happy. He had organized his spending carefully and was advancing professionally to where he was finally able to give up his night job. Janet was a free spirit. Her previous relationship was with an angry, controlling, and at times physically abusive man, and she was determined that no one would ever again bring her down like that. She wanted to have a good time and feel young again. Peter couldn't believe that such a beautiful, talented, funny, and vivacious woman could love him, but love him she did. Janet saw Peter as not only an attractive man who knew how to work hard and treat her well but also as a sort of anchor when she felt she was moving too fast. She felt safe with him. He helped her with some credit card problems she had developed, and she helped him learn to enjoy life a little.

By the time they came to see me, Peter had taken to calling Janet an "airhead." When Janet referred to her hard-working hubby, she had been heard to mutter "tight-ass" under her breath. Both felt hurt and betrayed by the fact that what their partner had once seen as essential and admirable elements of their characters were suddenly being viewed as fatal flaws.

What makes us resort to the most primitive, aggressive behavior against the same individuals whom we once cherished? What moves us to launch an attack on the once treasured qualities of the person to whom we have most intimately bound ourselves?

THE FIGHT-OR-FLIGHT RESPONSE: INTRODUCING THE REPTILIAN BRAIN

If you want to understand why (and how) you fight the one you love, you need to understand that it's only natural—if you look at it from a physical perspective. When you get into an argument with someone, you immediately—and unconsciously—tap into primitive bodily functions. Biological reactions to pain and stress create the foundation of most negative human interactions, even those occurring between lovers. When you understand this concept, you can understand any couple's mutually self-destructive, even sadistic behavior.

Our bodies are equipped with an instinctual reflexive system called the *fight-or-flight response*,[1] which is designed to protect us from harm. When we sense that we're being threatened, our bodies engage this powerful response system instantly, aimed toward one thing and one thing only—survival. We have only one immediate imperative: fight or run away.

Our entire body is affected, including physical and mental functioning. We experience shallow breathing, increased heart rate, change in blood flow, tightening of muscles (preparation to spring into action), heightened adrenaline production, and increased activity of neurotransmitters.[2] So complex and arousing is this state that one might say that we are actually most alive, physiologically speaking, when we're in a state of danger.

As all these physiological changes take place, what are we thinking?

Not much.

The Reptilian Response

As the body prepares for combat or to flee from a threat, the brain is making adjustments for the most efficient response by narrowing its focus and demands. A primitive portion of the brain, the *Reptilian Brain*, takes over primary responsibilities. The Reptilian Brain controls much of what we see as physical needs: breath, heart rate, muscle tension, physical aspects of sexual response, and self-protection through the aforementioned fight-or-flight response. The Reptilian Brain responds instinctually to the environment, enabling us to operate at about the same basic level as does a reptile. A reptile primarily eats, sleeps, fights, flees, and has sex. It can respond rapidly to protect itself from danger, but it does not have access to higher levels of cognitive functioning. When we're in a state of high stress or danger, our Reptilian Brain becomes our command center; it is concerned only with the immediate threat (real or perceived) to our safety and survival. We lose creativity, organizational skills, empathy, concentration, and ability to learn new information in direct proportion to the intensity of the stress.[3]

The concept of the fight-or-flight response holds that when threatened, any creature has two main options: (1) to fight back, attacking with the full intention of rendering the attacker harmless through injury or death, or (2) to attempt to run away or remain still, hoping the danger will pass by. All responses to threat fall into these two categories. Check the lists here to see if you recognize your favorite *modus operandi* during conflict. (You will notice that you might use fight and flight tactics simultaneously, such as attacking your partner and then trying to get away.)

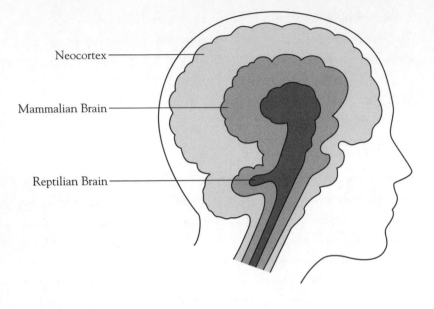

Neocortex

Mammalian Brain

Reptilian Brain

Flight

- Pretending you don't hear negative comments being made by your partner

- Leaving whenever conflict appears to be developing

- Avoiding bringing up any of your own concerns, because "it will just start something"

- Terminating any discussion that becomes uncomfortable by leaving or by saying, "I won't talk about this anymore!"

- Agreeing with your partner simply to be left alone

Fight

- Calling your partner names

- Threatening your partner with divorce, harm, property damage

- Using sarcasm

- Yelling or moving in a threatening, intimidating fashion

- Bringing up old behaviors as a way of driving home your point

- Physically abusing your partner, anything from pushing and shoving to serious violence

- Needing to win at all cost

The Reptile in the Modern World

You might think that as evolved human beings, we no longer need this primitive response system. However, the fight-or-flight response and the Reptilian Brain from which it comes are truly miraculous. If you're in a situation of physical threat, such as a potential car accident, you desperately need this system to work as it does.

Picture this: You're driving down the street in your neighborhood. You feel safe and comfortable because you know this area well. You are on the main straightaway, and you're almost home. Suddenly a car approaches from a side street. There is a stop sign that the other driver has apparently ignored. You barely have time to brake, turn your wheel, and avoid the collision.

In an instant, your fight-or-flight response took over and responded in rote mechanical ways that you, as an experienced driver, know well. What would have happened if this process had misfired and your higher-level brain had taken over? What if you had suddenly focused on trying to figure out exactly how hard you needed to hit the brake or how far to turn the wheel? What would have been your fate if you had become preoccupied with thoughts about why the other driver did such a stupid, reckless thing? You would have been injured or killed. Mercifully this does not happen. The Reptilian Brain takes over as a protective device without your needing to think about it. For a moment in time, perhaps nanoseconds, you don't care about anything intellectual—beauty, art, music, or philosophy. You don't care about what you plan to do when you get home. You don't care about the other driver, including whether he lives or dies. Your body's immediate self-protective reaction takes over and is nearly perfect. The Reptilian Brain has done its job.[4]

What happens, though, when another form of threat, such as a marital disagreement, arouses this same physical response?

THREAT AND DANGER IN A RELATIONSHIP: IT'S ALL IN HOW YOU SEE IT

In a very strict monastery, only one monk is allowed to speak on the first day of each month. Each is given a turn. On one occasion, the monk chosen for the part announced, "I don't like the mashed potatoes here. They're lumpy and tasteless." On the following month, another monk announced, "I like the mashed potatoes here. They always seem well-prepared and fresh." A month later, the third monk stood and proclaimed, "I'm leaving the monastery. I can't stand all this bickering."

Does arguing with your spouse really pose a threat to your life? After all, most people don't physically harm each other. So why does the Reptilian Brain kick in during a disagreement about who needs to take out the garbage? Each of us discerns the degree of threat based on a wide variety of inputs, including our current health, our level of stress, recent events, family history, culture, and many other issues. To understand the threats to a relationship, we must examine the various layers of the partners' interactions. You will see that in stressful situations, we tend to think oversimplistically and to reduce complex issues to the lowest common denominator.

Under severe threat, the Reptilian Brain overrides the higher-order mammalian and neocortical brains (which allow us to make more thoughtful decisions) and pushes us around in the "thoughtless" manner described earlier. In our relationships, we of course hope for higher-order thinking of the neocortical variety to help us make smart decisions and use logical problem-solving skills. Unfortunately, the Reptilian Brain often gets in the way.

Intimate human interaction is a complex beast indeed; however, the Reptilian Brain makes only the simplest choices. The Reptilian Brain doesn't organize data. Abstract or complex reasoning is foreign to it. It is not creative, nor does it empathize. It's not good at planning for the future, nor at predicting consequences. The Reptilian Brain decides merely, "Should I eat it, kill it, run away from it, or have sex with it?"

The chart here describes the thinking skills involved at the different levels of brain function,[5] using as an example possible responses to meeting someone for the first time:

Thinking Skill	*Response to New Acquaintance*
New Brain (Neocortex)—Understanding past experience and planning for the future, reasoning and science, abstract reasoning	Can I trust this person? This person seems attractive, but do I know enough about him or her? Are we similar enough in values, beliefs, and tastes to really have a good relationship?
Mammalian Brain—Pursuing affection, engaging in family and social ties, responding to sense of duty and responsibility	Will this person really care for and love me? Am I safe with him or her? This person seems smart and kind, and I'm sure I feel something here.
Reptilian Brain—Eating, sleeping, fighting, running away, mating	I really, really, really want to have sex with this person.

Physically, the Reptilian Brain is located very close to those parts of our brain that govern speech. Unfortunately, we can be quite verbal without being able to access our best thinking faculties. There is much wisdom in the slogan, "Caution: Please ensure that brain is engaged before opening mouth."[6]

The fight-or-flight response evokes black-or-white thinking. The brain narrows its focus to survival necessities. Higher brain functioning, such as abstract reasoning—your ability to understand metaphors, representations, jokes, and other communications requiring interpretation—is diminished. A remark that once might have been shrugged off or seen as amusing is now experienced as a poison dart thrown right at your heart. You are more easily confused and therefore more easily threatened.

How often have you been in a battle where you and your partner could not stay on a single point? As you fought, you each used hurtful memories or episodes, no matter how vague or ancient, as a way of saying that your partner was wrong, stupid, offensive, or evil. You could not stay focused and maintain a reasonable discussion because the Reptilian Brain doesn't have organizational skills. Have you ever referred to your partner, in the heat of battle, in a sarcastic, demeaning, or obscene way, one in which you would never address any other person, not even an enemy? At some level, you know that this will be hurtful and make your partner feel terrible. You know that the person you love should not be treated this way. Yet your Reptilian Brain cannot reason in this fashion. It cannot empathize or fully appreciate the likely results of combative behavior.

We often treat strangers better than we treat those closest to us. This isn't because we like strangers better than our loved ones, nor because "familiarity breeds contempt." It's because we place the highest expectations on those closest to us, and consequently risk the greatest disappointments in such relationships. An intimate relationship is the safest, most rewarding place for us when it is good and the most dangerous place when it has soured. Strangers cannot harm us as deeply as those we truly care about. We have an imagined agreement with our loved ones; we expect to be loved, admired, lusted after, and enjoyed, no matter how poorly we may behave. The discovery that no human being can always live up to these expectations creates a deep wound.

How Important Is Safety in Intimacy?

In a verbal battle, the level of perceived threat relates to your relationship with the other combatant and to your immediate needs. Do you need this person to agree with you, do business with you, not feel superior to you, love and care for you? Does this person make you feel safe? In love relationships, safety is essential. Without a sense of safety, we're more likely to go into the reptilian mode and attack our loved one.[7] The threat is not necessarily one of physical harm (we'll discuss physical violence later), but to our sense of well-being and to our need to be okay, competent, powerful, and loved. When a loved one—probably the most influential person in your life—attacks you or somehow implies a lack of caring, love, or respect for you, you quickly perceive emotional threat and the need to protect yourself.

REPTILES IN LOVE

The Frightened Monster

Married for fifteen years, and now complaining that they have nothing in common, Tom and Anita are stuck. They argue about who spends money more foolishly and whose hobbies are the bigger waste of time. They complain that even when they have something very important to discuss, they never really solve anything. Tom complains that Anita won't stick with a discussion, and she states that the only way that he'll be satisfied is if she just gives in and agrees with him.

(continued on next page)

(continued)

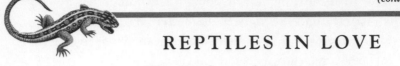

REPTILES IN LOVE

The Frightened Monster

Tom is a large, muscular man with a deep, booming voice that is a little loud even in casual discussion. Anita is a petite woman who tends to look down at the floor when she's making her more assertive points. As they portray their interactions in exquisite detail, Anita insists that she often becomes afraid of Tom. When Tom hears this, he becomes red in the face and demands that Anita admit that he has "never touched her." During this discussion he has considerable difficulty sitting still. He leans forward, raises his voice, and finally says, "I've had it. Nothing I do is right, and you just keep running away. Maybe we should just get a divorce."

Tom has no intention of harming Anita. He can't believe that she would think he could. Anita can't stand the tone and volume of his voice and the physical intimidation he displays when angry and frustrated. She describes him standing up in such arguments, stepping toward her, and overpowering whatever she says with his loud voice. Whenever it looks like a discussion is headed in this direction, she tries to get away from him. Her attempts at escape frustrate and threaten Tom. The more she flees, the more helpless and fearful he becomes. The more helpless he feels, the more reptilian his responses become. Shouting and intimidating has never gotten Anita to agree with him, but when he's most frightened, he's unable to see this. He comes across as a bully. She can't understand how he can treat her so poorly.

Tom and Anita have developed a perfect cycle of danger and frustration. Each accuses the other of not listening . . . and both are right. The Reptilian Brain cannot listen accurately; in order to hear each other and respond in a helpful way, they must be able to calm themselves and slow things down. Their brains would then begin to work properly, and the higher-level functions would kick in. Instead, they both feel that they must solve the problem before they can calm down—but they can't solve *anything* until they can listen to each other. To listen to each other, they must first calm down. Thus, the cycle continues.

Evolutionary Tip
Quick Release from
Reptilian Responses

Perhaps the most difficult challenge you face in working on your relationship is recognizing when the Reptilian Brain is about to strike, and cutting off your own physiological arousal before it overwhelms you. The earlier you intervene with the fight-or-flight response, the less damage will occur. Starting now, I suggest you take the following actions as you begin working on your relationship. This is a first step in reducing the destructive patterns in your difficult interactions. (The process will become clearer as you learn more about yourself and your relationship.)

1. *Monitor yourself for reptilian responses.* (These include racing heart, muscle tension, desire to escape, desire to defend yourself, desire to defeat your partner.)

2. *Take a deep "abdominal" breath or two.* (Inhale slowly through your nose, first inflating your abdomen (it looks like a beer belly but it works), then expand your chest and finally raise your shoulders in order to let the last bit of air into your lungs. Hold the breath briefly and exhale slowly through your mouth, reversing the process above, first

(continued on next page)

Evolutionary Tip
**Quick Release from
Reptilian Responses** (*continued*)

releasing your shoulders, deflating your chest, and finally feeling your abdomen release. Feel tension release as you exhale and then repeat.)

3. *Now ask yourself two questions:* *

   a. What is this discussion about?

   b. What do I need right now?

   *As you progress through the book, you may wish to ask your partner what he or she sees as the goal of the discussion and what he or she needs right now.

4. If you feel that you are still negatively aroused and unable to have a good discussion, stop and *take a break for at least twenty minutes*. Leave the room, maybe even leave the house and go for a walk or run around the block. (You and your partner will eventually discover how long these breaks actually need to be, but it generally takes the body at least twenty minutes to recover from the fight-or-flight state.)

Whenever you feel your Reptilian Brain taking over (and as you read through the book, you'll recognize it more and more), practice this Quick Release from Reptilian Responses. I'll remind you about it at various points as we go on.

Can Anita feel safe? Tom has never physically harmed her and probably never will. But when her personal space is being invaded, such empirical data don't mean squat. Her Reptilian Brain takes over, and all she can focus on is getting out of the situation. Tom is hovering over her, yelling, wanting, and waiting. Why? And for what? As she sees it, she can gain relief only by physically leaving the room or by "surrendering" to Tom (which is a form of escape).

Does Tom feel safe? Anita has certainly never physically harmed him. Yet when she pulls away from him, he feels ignored, put down, unloved, and even treated as if he were dangerous or despicable. This from the person who used to claim she loved him! The only way he can get relief is to get her to sit still and hear him out. He will say, "She doesn't have to agree with me, but for God's sake, she could at least listen to me now and then."

Lovers in battle are like gunslingers. Once a showdown has started and injuries have been inflicted, both partners have armed themselves. To move closer to one another, each must put down his or her weapons. Imagine if, in the Old West, two gunslingers faced off in the street and one of them said, "Hey, I'll tell you what. I'll just keep my gun aimed at your chest while you put yours down. After you've done that, I promise to put mine down as well." The response, of course, would be something along the lines of "Bite me!" Once betrayed—by harsh words or inappropriate behavior—neither partner can feel safe. It's just that simple. You don't need to draw blood or leave a bruise to inflict an injury.

Opposites Attract—and Fight in Opposite Ways

Tom and Anita, like many other couples, argue often. For them, it's not the number of arguments that is the problem, it's that they have such diametrically opposite fighting styles. Their family histories and traditions help us understand their differences.

Tom comes from a boisterous family of rowdies, in which the dinner table has all the calm and decorum of the bleachers at Wrigley Field. Disagreement and battle are a standing family tradition and are not seen as detracting at all from the family members' affection for one another. For them, silence and retreat are actually signs of disdain.

Anita comes from a quiet, well-mannered family, one that keeps disagreements to a minimum and frowns on raised voices. Family members show care for one another through many acts of kindness, touching, and hugging, and they feel confused by arguments. They engage in earnest discussion of the issues and strive toward compromise, and they all appreciate the warmth of the home. It all feels kind of nice to Tom, but sometimes a little creepy too. When things are good, he seems to enjoy Anita's family. When he's angry, he refers to them as the Cleavers, intoning the name as warmly as one might the Manson family.

As a young woman, Anita found her home safe but a little boring. She appreciated Tom's more lively behavior and "the way he laughed and carried on." Tom liked the quiet and thoughtful woman he found in Anita. She made him feel calmer. Now Anita sometimes feels completely overrun, if not threatened, by Tom, and Tom feels that she is avoiding and ignoring him. Both feel more and more hopeless about ever feeling respected by the other.

Evolutionary Tip
Recognize Dangerous Partners

Warning!

Although our goal is to help partners help each other slow down the patterns of the fight-or-flight response, the reality is that some partners are indeed dangerous. If your partner has used physical violence or threats of violence to you, your family, or your children; threats to take your children away; threats to have you arrested on imaginary charges; or threats of damage to your property, read no further. You absolutely must see to your safety before you can continue to work on your relationship. I will not continue in therapy with a couple who has experienced physical violence or threats of violence without a commitment by both that they will take all steps necessary to ensure their mutual safety. At worst, separation may be necessary, but in most cases we have been able to reach other agreements that allow the couple to stay together with a guarantee from both partners of no further physical contact or dangerous behavior when upset.

For any couple to come to cooperate and grow close, both parties must feel safe. A husband who has pushed or struck his wife might commit to avoiding any hint of threatening behavior, such as agreeing to remain seated throughout discussions in their home. If this becomes impossible, he will end the discussion and remove himself for a prescribed amount of time to calm down. In return, the wife may agree that at such times, she will not pursue him and try to "finish" the fight. Notice, please, that at the point where he's feeling as though he can't sit still and she can't stop arguing, this is no longer a discussion or disagreement: it's a *fight*. As long as they remain in the reptilian mode, the possibility that either of them will learn something new or reach a positive solution is nearly zero. Their agreement may also include that if one of them simply cannot control himself or herself, the other will call the police.

Confusing? I'm warning you to protect yourself. I'm also asking you to be open to change. We keep coming back to trust and honesty. If you can't trust your partner not to seriously injure you, your family, your possessions, your reputation, or your well-being, then it's impossible to work on improving your relationship. If you can gradually devise agreements that allow you to feel safe in the situation, then communication and increased intimacy stand a chance. It's not all that confusing, is it?

The subject of safety is much broader than implied by the dramatic examples I've presented. Often when I initially describe safety issues with couples, they think that I mean exclusively physical safety, and therefore feel exempt because "Oh, we don't have those problems." But safety also means the freedom from feeling insulted, ignored, rejected, controlled, unloved, or in any other way diminished as a person. Safety includes freedom from feeling like a bad, stupid, or incompetent partner. My goal is to encourage you to provide that kind of safety to one another.

Working out safety issues requires a great deal of faith, trust, and sensitivity, which is probably already lacking when a couple is angry, volatile, or disconnected. Suppose I tell you that when you start yelling, I'm afraid you'll hurt me. You (who don't have any intention of hurting me) may feel that I'm exaggerating or attempting to paint you in a bad light. So you try to convince me that I'm treating you unfairly. When you see that I'm still afraid, you become frustrated and start yelling at me. It doesn't really matter what you say next, because I disconnected the minute you started yelling.

If Tom can recognize that Anita becomes physically upset and is unable to focus when he gets loud or moves toward her, he can experiment with changing his behavior. He doesn't have to admit to being a bad or intimidating person. And Anita would do well not to use terminology that negatively categorizes Tom. Calling him a bully, a big jerk, or a loudmouthed blowhard could be taken the wrong way, after all.

Think about it another way. If Tom wore cologne, which he liked but that nauseated Anita, he would probably stop wearing that cologne. In the same way, if he could see that his in-your-face behavior, which seems perfectly reasonable to him, upsets Anita, he would stop "wearing" his aggression in her presence.

Tom and Anita might agree to have their most serious discussions at the dining room table. Tom will be less likely to advance on Anita with a table between them, and, although attack is still possible, Anita may just feel a little safer. They might agree on a "ten-foot rule" that requires them to maintain ten feet between them when discussing anything serious. If they really want to be playful, they can measure out a ten-foot length of rope and hold it taut between them. If the rope goes slack, they need to take a break in the discussion. I have even had a few large, overwhelming men sit on the floor while talking to their wives, who remain sitting in a chair. This changes the dynamics dramatically.

The Greatest Fear of All

An elderly woman is sitting in a rocking chair and petting her cat, when suddenly a fairy appears and proclaims, "You have led a good life, and I will grant you three wishes."

*The woman says, "I want to be twenty-four years old and
beautiful once again."*

*The fairy says, "Let it be," and sure enough the woman
is transformed into a young beauty.*

*Next, the woman wishes for a million dollars, and imme-
diately this is granted. Finally she says, "I wish my old cat
here were a handsome young man who would fall deeply in
love with me."*

*Poof. She finds herself in the arms of the best-looking
guy she has ever seen in her life, and he is looking at her
adoringly.*

*He kisses her gently and says, "I'll bet you wish you hadn't
had me fixed."*

The one thing it seems everyone fears most in relationships is change.
(As in the joke here, even the most seemingly alluring changes can
disappoint or harm.) Why is change so frightening? What keeps
couples from trying counseling or other interventions when they hit
a bad patch? How can there be so much resistance when it seems
clear that improving their relationship would have such immediate
benefits?

The following are common fears most people face when attempting major changes in their relationships:

- Nothing will happen.

- Things will improve, but only for a short time, and
  then we'll go back to the same rut, back to doing the
  same old things that hurt so much before, but we'll
  feel worse.

- Things will get better, but it won't be enough. My
  partner will try to please me, and I still won't be
  happy; (or) I'll work hard and make myself vulnerable,

and it won't be enough. Either way, I'll really feel like a jerk.

- I'll be asked to do things that won't be good for me or that I can't do.

- Things could get worse. Right now our relationship may not be great, but it's okay, and if we muck around with it, who knows what might happen?

Recognizing and discussing these perfectly normal fears may speed you along to some of the most pressing matters in your relationship. Kept as secrets, they can be fatal to the change process and to the relationship.

Obviously there's risk in any change, and any request for change is stressful at some level. The request suggests that something is wrong, which is stressful in its own right. But what if your request is for something your partner doesn't really believe he or she can do? The partner's answer might be, "I don't need to change. There's nothing wrong with a drink or two (or twenty) in the evening." But the truth the partner holds back may be, "I don't think I can do this. How am I supposed to give up alcohol when I feel so awful?" Other examples include requests that a quiet person talk more or be more outgoing, that a sloppy person be neater, that an angry person stop being so angry, that a person upset with the partner's family treat them better—and the list goes on. Acknowledging the partner's fear that he or she can't make a change allows the couple to back up and look at what part of the request is negotiable or how the change can be made more manageable.

The thread throughout these fears is the hopelessness that one or both partners experience with one another and the sense that, through the change process, they will be made to feel even worse than they already do. These fears must be respected and addressed. When one partner's reptilian response to a request for change is

"Get off my back! Why are you always nagging me? Did you learn about marriage in a concentration camp?" what he might really mean is "I'm afraid to try to change. What if I can't do it? I'm afraid that if I can't change, you'll leave me." This can be an extremely painful admission, but it can also be tremendously freeing once acknowledged.

———————

Now that you've been introduced to the Reptilian Brain, you should have a clearer understanding of why you fight with people you love. In the next chapter, we'll take a closer look at some of the things we actually fight about and the "stupid" ways we go about it.

2

Lizard Madness

Understanding Methods and Cycles in Stupid Fighting

All cruelty springs from weakness.

Seneca

What's with this Reptilian Brain, anyway? The positive side is that it pushes me out of the way of speeding cars and saves me from being eaten by wild animals. The negative side is that it persuades me to react as if my partner were a speeding car or wild animal when all she said was, "Honey, can you take the kids to school today?" Next thing you know, we're off to the races, and the day is filled with fights about stupid stuff.

This chapter is about the "stuff" that riles our Reptilian Brains, the stupid fighting that ensues, and how we can disengage from the cycles of stupidity with which we damage ourselves and our relationships.

Please don't feel insulted by the term *stupid fighting*. I hope that by now you've joined me in the assumption that when we're stressed out, we're all a little stupid. In this state, we're prone to make huge errors in our interpretation of events around us. We may perceive a threat or attack that was never intended. We then feel a desperate need to defend ourselves, which may not at all fit the situation and which our partner will perceive as unprovoked and unwarranted. He or she will respond out of feelings of shame and betrayal, and behold, the battle is on.[1]

In literature, as in many other aspects of our culture, we often hear comparisons between substance and style. Substance refers to what is actually being presented, and style is the manner in which the presentation is made. In therapy, the terminology is different, but the concept is the same; we talk about the difference between content and process. The content of an argument consists of the facts and opinions being discussed at the moment. Process is how the argument started, how it is being fought, how it ends, and other data about how things are taking place. An important process question is "Why now?" In other words, why is this act of aggression happening right now? What do the partners need from each other? If they're arguing over whether one of them was being sarcastic or not, the content is whether sarcasm occurred. If the partners discuss only this fact, then more important questions may be lost: whether one partner intended to be hostile and whether the other is feeling hurt, as two possibilities.

If you're like most couples, you might notice that much of what you fight about is nonsense. For example:

I work a lot harder than you do.

You're ruining us financially!

You're too cheap!

It's your mother's fault.

You're a rotten parent.

I'm smarter than you.

It's your hormones (or some other health issue).

You're too sensitive.

I know what you're thinking.

If you really loved me, you'd know what I was thinking.

What you might not notice is that the nonsense covers up more important issues that may be perceived as too dangerous to discuss or of which you and your partner have no conscious awareness. These arguments are driven more by competition and Reptilian Brain functioning than by healthy needs.[2]

I submit that the real topic of discussion underlying all the nonsense is "Do you really care about, love, and respect me?" or "Am I safe with you?" or both. Think about the last argument you had with your lover. Suppose that instead of continuing to argue over the minutiae of the battle, you suddenly stopped and said, "Right now I'm feeling as though you don't like me very much. Is that true?" Might this change things? If your partner answered truthfully as to whether he or she cares about you or is too angry to enjoy you right now, the two of you might enter into a richer, more personal interaction.[3] Sadly, we often remain in a competitive stance, in which we try hard to *win*, making guesses or trying to outwit each other and ultimately, as in the joke here, investing in the wrong efforts.

> *Over breakfast one morning, a woman said to her husband, "I bet you don't know what day this is."*
>
> *"Of course I do," he indignantly answered, going out the door to his office.*
>
> *At 10 A.M., the doorbell rang, and when the woman opened the door, she was handed a box containing a dozen long-stemmed red roses. At 1 P.M., a foil-wrapped, two-pound box of her favorite chocolates arrived. Later, a boutique delivered a designer dress. The woman couldn't wait for her husband to come home.*
>
> *"First the flowers, then the chocolates, and then the dress!" she exclaimed. "I've never had a more wonderful Groundhog Day in all my life!"*

To illustrate what happens in stupid fighting, let's explore three of the most common fighting styles.

STUPID FIGHTING STYLE 1:
BICKER, BICKER, BICKER

One of the most frequent manifestations of stupid fighting is constant bickering—couples who take jabs at each other at every opportunity. Often they fight about the same things over and over again. The following are three "hot" topics I hear repeatedly in therapy:

1. Let's blame your family.
2. I know exactly what you're going to do before you do it.
3. If you really loved me, you'd know what I need.

Let's Blame Your Family

A really nasty way in which we attack each other is by using insider information about our partner's family. We take information, perhaps confided to us during times of trust and camaraderie, and turn it against our partner. This is a terrible betrayal. It never works, and it always leaves a mark. "You act just like your father." "All the women in your family nag and bitch as a hobby." "If your mother hadn't babied you, maybe you could hold a decent job."

These attacks will always put your partner on the defensive. We absolutely must defend our families because they're part of us, and in defending them we're also protecting ourselves. Let me emphasize this point: if you insist on attacking your partner's family in a confrontation, you are deciding to harm your relationship. Your partner's reptilian response will be to protect her family—even if she agrees with you.

The double tragedy of attacking a partner's family is that your partner may have his own concerns, anger, or sadness about his family. Once you've chosen to attack in this way, you remove yourself as a trusted confidant. When your partner is angry at or hurt by something that a parent or sibling has done, will he be able to turn to you for help? If he has had to defend his family against you, it's not bloody likely!

What to Do

When you find yourself attacking your partner's family, practice the Quick Release from Reptilian Responses, described in Chapter One. Then make an agreement with your partner that families are off-limits for discussion, at least for a period of time, until you're able to speak of them more respectfully. The subject is simply too dangerous and too likely to bring on a reptilian response.

When you bring up your partner's family, you're usually trying to give evidence of your partner's behavior, or even trying to excuse it. Instead, tell your partner what you need and focus on the specific behavior you would like to have changed. (You'll understand more about dealing with each other's families as you complete some assessments about your families' differences in Chapter Three.)

I Know Exactly What You're Going to Do Before You Do It

In this battle, you assume your partner will always act in a predictable way, irrespective of your needs. Patterns may have established themselves to the point that there is some accuracy in your predictions, but they still don't really invite your partner to be of help to you. If you say, for instance, "I know that when we go to that party, you're going to ignore me and spend all your time with other people," you already place your loved one on the defensive as the kind of person who ignores his partner. Even if this is true, it's hard for your partner to listen to, because it predicts an offense that has not yet occurred. Predicting the future is very risky business. Instead of inviting change, the partner's Reptilian Brain often eggs him on to even worse behavior ("I'll show her—let's ignore her completely tonight!").

What to Do

If you fear that you'll be abandoned at the party, ask for a specific change in behavior. This allows your partner to give you something rather than forcing him to argue his positive traits with you. So you might want to say instead, "I would really feel better if you would check in with me every half hour or so during the party. Sometimes I feel pretty ignored at those things."

Your partner can now respond to something you want. Of course, this is useful only if you can trust your partner to want to help you. If this is in doubt, then the two of you need to discuss your fear that he doesn't care. Often, however, the partner does want to help but isn't sure how to do so.

If You Really Loved Me, You'd Know What I Need

If we don't want our partners to predict our behavior or define us, then we shouldn't expect them to read our minds. Obviously, the more relaxed and connected a couple is, the more often they will experience those magic moments when they really do understand each other's needs. Too often, though, partners see mind-reading as some kind of barometer as to how connected they really are. Personally, I believe in the magic of relationships—but I also believe that it's a matter of respect to tell your partner what you need from her and not to test her by withholding information.

Everyone wants to think her partner is her "soul mate" and that this soulfully connected person will clearly understand and meet her needs. Unfortunately, the concept of the soul mate is not particularly helpful. It implies a magical selection of one person who is a spiritual guarantee of relationship success. I'm a little jaded because it seems as though I most often hear the term "soul mate" from people describing an extramarital affair or a very short relationship. There should be a rule that you have to be together successfully for about fifteen years before you can use this term—and then only sparingly.

Successful relationships involve two people striving to understand, respect, and support each other. When partners succeed in this effort, relationships are indeed spiritually rewarding. It is not the other way around. There is no great lottery in life in which, if you find the right soul mate, you can sit back and enjoy the benefits. If you believe that your lover is a perfect soul mate (and that implies perfect agreement and 100 percent positive interactions), you're doomed. Such an idea leads to a terrible sense of betrayal when you find out that no two people can be everything to each other and so must eventually disappoint.

What to Do

The soul mate dream is a romantic fantasy that most of us are reluctant to relinquish. It's also the wish for perfect caretaking, and that's impossible. If you feel injured because your partner doesn't attend to you the way you wish or because you define intimacy as your partner's being able to guess what you desire, then you'll have to change your focus. Ask yourself what kind of comfort or reassurance you need from your partner. Do you have trouble asking for what you need? Are you afraid that your request won't be granted? It might not be. But if your needs are rejected or ignored after you ask for them to be met, you then have the opportunity to deal with the situation directly rather than hiding behind the "he should just know" defense. However, odds are that your partner is simply not aware of what you want him to do.

STUPID FIGHTING STYLE 2: ANYTHING YOU CAN DO . . .

Humans strive for power to overcome and compensate for inevitable childhood feelings of inferiority, impotence and dependence on adults.

Alfred Adler

Our idea of the "ideal" relationship is made up of two people who "complete" each other (as Jerry Maguire would say), who are the yin to each other's yang. They would therefore respect and appreciate what each one brings to the relationship.

In the real world, however, couples often get caught up in trying to outdo (outwork, outplay, outlove, outparent) each other. The struggle for power can become a day-to-day preoccupation.

Although many couples are reluctant to discuss competition and control as aspects of their relationship, these are among the most common and necessary of defenses. It's through competition that we gain and develop skills and abilities. We discover areas in which we are competent, maybe even the best. We discover the thrill of feeling effective and skilled, and the danger of being overwhelmed by an opponent. We demonstrate our skills, attractiveness, and efficacy as a way of attracting sexual partners. The initial means of attracting and attempting to maintain a relationship are quite primitive and appeal to reptilian and mammalian instincts.

One might even suggest that the placing of rings, tattoos, and names (both informal, as in nicknames like Snuggy-muffin and Babykins, and formal, as in taking on family names in marriage) is a way of exerting a degree of control over a sexual partner. We want to know that this person will be there for us, and our anxiety about this leads us to label or mark him or her as ours. Such demonstrations of commitment are important as statements to each other and to the external world that we are partners. We have chosen each other and do not have to repeatedly face that uncertainty. We have won and can move on to new adventures. So what happens when that security is threatened?

The Competition (or I'd Rather Be Right Than Get Laid)

A middle-aged guy walked into a bar and sat down with a big smile on his face. The bartender said, "Hey, it's good to see a guy in a good mood in here. What's going on?"

The patron giggled and replied, "After all these years I'm finally taller than my big brother."

"What do you mean?" the bartender asked. "You can't still be growing at your age."

"Oh, no. My brother was in a bad accident today. They had to amputate his legs."

The most dramatic representation of "fight" in the reptilian fight-or-flight response is the drive to defeat one's opponent, to compete. Although you may not consciously think of your partner as an opponent, the drive to score points in your relationship is a primitive function, related to an innate drive for safety. You developed your perceptions of and responses to this need early in life, in your family of origin. Partners usually discover in therapy that they're applying old defenses to their new relationship. The rules and roles they learned as children or in previous relationships no longer apply, but they keep trying. Competing with your partner doesn't necessarily mean that you don't care about him or her, but simply that you can't allow yourself to relax and show caring—because that might suggest weakness. In fact, destructive competition in a relationship is a weakness, not a sign of strength.

REPTILES IN LOVE
The Loyal Opposition

Victor and Suzanne talked to me about the competitive battles they would have over the most mundane topics. For example, at a store, Suzanne parallel parked on a side street. Victor noted that she did a fine job, since they were at least within walking distance of the curb. Suzanne then reminded Victor that she wasn't the one with traffic tickets, whereas he appeared to be accumulating a rather fine and

(continued on next page)

(continued)

REPTILES IN LOVE

The Loyal Opposition

extensive collection. The "Who Is the Better Driver" battle was in play, a competition they could wage for considerable amounts of time without ever really saying anything of value. Suzanne went on to say that Victor seemed to have a smart remark about anything she did, and she was really getting sick of it. Victor defended himself by stating that Suzanne didn't have a sense of humor and that in fact this lack of a comedy gene was pervasive throughout her family.

What role does competition play in this relationship? For Victor it may be as simple as a bad personality habit that requires him to defeat people linguistically. It may also serve as a means of maintaining some distance; often sarcasm, criticism, and other forms of competition are means of regulating intimacy between two parties. That's why simply encouraging the partners to stop such behaviors does not work.

Suzanne eventually developed a "policy of nonengagement" that actually allowed them to engage. She would respond to almost any taunt by Victor with a standard phrase, such as "Do you really want to criticize me for that right now? Is it important for us to talk about that?" In quieter times, she did confront Victor with how much his comments hurt her and pushed her away from him.[4] This then led to more discussion of other aspects of their intimacy that were disappearing. Victor began to examine his need to treat Suzanne with disdain and agreed to do some individual therapy. For his part, he felt that Suzanne had every guy in town ogling her, so her self-esteem shouldn't be an issue. She was eventually able to convince him that other guys staring at her did not make her feel confident at all.

Sometimes partners feel the need for battle as a means of keeping each other at a nonintrusive distance. It's critical to remember that partners have differing needs and tolerances for closeness, and many have trouble regulating such intimacy needs and limitations effectively. It strikes many as odd that they are having trouble tolerating the closeness of their partner, even though it has become quite chic to assert, "I need my space." Once people are able to talk comfortably about their specific needs, such as a little time to themselves to read or a night out with friends, the pressure to distance in dysfunctional ways will dissipate. (If I don't need to defend myself against you or to compete with you, then I also don't need to keep you at bay in an unhealthy fashion. I can even trust you to leave me alone if I request that, and we'll still be okay.)

A more extreme level of this competitive need is seen in the need for control over the partner. Let's look at this particular issue more directly.

The Need for Control (or I'm Always Right, Whether You're Wrong or Not)

In response to a threat (real or perceived), we often are driven to control our environment. Comparatively healthy manifestations of this drive might include making lists or doing lots of planning and down-to-the-minute scheduling. Unhealthy manifestations might include the need to control a loved one's thoughts and behaviors. In the early stages of a relationship, controlling behavior is often mistaken for caring attentiveness, when in fact it is at best a response to anxiety.

The need for control takes on many forms, but let's examine one common form: jealousy.

> A wife was so jealous that she constantly tried to catch her husband in a lie. She had become so preoccupied with this idea that when he came home late one night, she instantly inspected his clothing for strange hairs and sniffed him to catch the scent of perfume. Finding nothing, she shouted, "Great! You're cheating on me with a bald woman who's too cheap to buy perfume!"

Jealousy is about the need to control, pure and simple. What most jealous partners don't like to hear is that jealousy is abusive.

REPTILES IN LOVE
Every Step You Take

Judy and Garth have been together for about five years and married for two. During their courtship, Garth was an absolute gentleman and always attentive. Judy thought of him as almost "puppylike," always wanting to be close to her. She knew he had a jealous streak and that he didn't like it when she talked to other guys, even if they were classmates or colleagues. When he saw her touch a colleague on the arm once while laughing at something, he questioned her about whether there was something going on. Generally these episodes didn't last long, and the good times they had more than made up for them.

Judy was surprised that Garth's possessiveness seemed to increase after they were married. She thought he would feel safer once they made their relationship formal. She was shocked when he wanted to review what she was going to wear to work every day. He would become intensely angry if she bought a new dress or even undergarments that he thought might make her too alluring. On the other hand, he wanted her to dress in a fairly provocative manner when they went out together (but then got upset if men looked at her). She got the mixed messages that he worshipped her beyond all reason and that she was a slut. This went on for two years, until she began seeing a counselor. She hadn't discussed her concerns with Garth because, she said, "He just doesn't get it. He thinks he's just showing me how much he cares. He doesn't realize how dirty I feel when he keeps checking on me."

This is a very dangerous situation for a relationship. The seething rage and exhaustion at constantly having to defend yourself leads to a burning out of all feelings. Often by the time a person seeks help, he's so deadened to his partner, so traumatized by the persistent questioning and control, he no longer feels anything. I've been told many times in such situations that "Even if she stopped all of this today, I don't think I would ever feel good around her again."

Ironically, an additional risk is that the aggression of the control, accusations, and questions actually leads to the most feared outcome. The victim of such controlling behavior finds someone else paying her positive attention, a person with whom she doesn't have to work so hard at defending herself, and, you guessed it, she falls in love. She's amazed at being liked and trusted and at how easy it is to get along with this new friend. The relief of this positive attention is far too enticing and the damage of jealousy too vast for her to even consider working on the original relationship.

Many forms of jealousy are very treatable.[5] In the treatment of anxious, obsessive persons, I encourage *both* partners to work on the problem. If the jealous partner simply can't get the questioning or accusations under control, even after recognizing the damage she's doing, it's likely that she's experiencing other symptoms of depression or anxiety as well. It will be important that the jealousy is recognized by both partners as a symptom of an illness that has little to do with their actual caring for one another. Such persons need treatment and often benefit from medication, and in the case of uncontrollable jealousy, medication may make the difference in whether the relationship survives.

Understanding this pattern as an illness may give the receiving partner some relief from the intense pain and anger that the mistrust arouses. However, treating this as an illness doesn't give a controlling partner a "blank check" to continue questioning and checking. He still must take responsibility for his actions and will need to work diligently on controlling the offending behaviors. It also means, however, that often the controlling partner is not doing this in a purposeful or evil manner but is truly out of control himself. In Chapter Eight I will discuss a very different aspect of control. When there has been some form of betrayal in the relationship, some controlling behaviors may be needed in order to provide the injured partner with some sense of safety.

STUPID FIGHTING STYLE 3: WE SUFFER IN SILENCE

The Minnesota couple was celebrating their fiftieth anniversary. The wife said, "You know, it just kind of bothers me that in all these years that we've been together, you never tell me that you love me."

Her husband seemed truly surprised and replied, "Now you know I told you I loved you when I asked you to marry me. If anything had changed in the meantime, I would have let you know."

Not all couples are warriors of words. Some don't participate in full-blown, angry, name-calling battles, but instead simply have little or no connection or communication left in their relationship. They're not actively fighting, but neither are they engaged in any other way. Their reptilian response is to flee—to get as far away as possible without physically leaving the relationship.

REPTILES IN LOVE
Now What Do We Do?

"She never wants to talk to me," Ben mumbled. He and Vicky were sitting on the loveseat (a peculiar name for furniture in a marital

session) in my office and had managed to leave a wide gap between themselves in spite of the small space.

"Do you know what he means by that?" I asked Vicky.

"I guess so," she replied with no further elaboration. We had just introduced ourselves, and I could tell that it was going to be a long forty-five minutes.

Ben and Vicky described their twelve-year relationship. They'd been married for ten-and-a-half of those years and had two lovely children on whom they both doted. Ben thought that the only mutual interest they still had was their children. They didn't seem to have anything else to talk about to each other. At one point in this description, Vicky snapped, "What are we supposed to talk about, politics?" It was her longest response of the session so far.

When I asked how they met and began their romance, Ben and Vicky spoke as if they had somehow just drifted into marriage. Ben had been encouraged by friends to ask Vicky out. Vicky thought Ben was a nice guy and didn't see any reason not to go out with him. Not too long into the relationship, they thought they should just go ahead, get married, and start a family. They both admitted having some reservations about the marriage but also felt that this is what people do at their age. Their families were thrilled with their decision. Coincidentally, both Vicky and Ben were told by their respective parents that they were *lucky* to get such a partner.

Ben and Vicky are what I call a *disconnected* couple. Connection is a difficult quality to define; there is no measure of how often people need to talk or touch in order to feel connected. Clearly, two people can be in separate parts of a room—not talking, each reading his or her own book—yet feel totally entwined with one another.

Conversely, partners can feel detached from one another in the middle of the sexual act. If you cannot answer yes to the question, "Do you ever feel close to each other?" then there is a problem.

Unfortunately, the couple who has disengaged can be more challenging than the engaged angry couple. Silent partners generally offer less energy to the change process. They don't really have disagreements to work through because they simply silence all discontent and desire, and make do. For their relationship to be revived, their ability to interact must be rebuilt.

For these couples, the traditional goals of marital therapy, such as increased enjoyment, connection, and intimacy, actually increase anxiety. It would seem to any observer (and to themselves as well) that they need to learn to have some fun together—to reignite their relationship. However, as soon as one or both of the partners perceive that they're being asked to talk more or to offer more to the relationship, they will retreat to an even more defeated and disengaged position.

The treatment goal in this case must be to reduce tension and anxiety, even though it seems paradoxical to work toward safety and calm in a couple that looks relationally comatose. It's essential to reduce the tension in order for them to reengage (more on improving such relationships in Chapter Six).

Passive-Aggressive Silence

If their silence is primarily linked to low self-esteem, partners may have trouble asking for what they need because they don't feel entitled to more than what they have. Many people have severe difficulties in asking for what they want. Because of this, many silent couples communicate through passive-aggressive behavior. Passive-aggression is a reptilian defense mechanism for dealing with negative, intolerable, and unapproachable thoughts or behaviors. If my wife asks me to do something and I don't want to do it—but I can't bring myself to tell her—I might forget to do it, do it poorly, or arrive too late to accomplish it. I don't plan to defeat her in this way, and I would never admit, even to myself, that my failure was purposeful in any way.

We all demonstrate passive-aggression to some degree in our lives, but when it is the primary defense, it can be devastating. Passive-aggressive behavior between partners serves to push them further apart, in ways they cannot usually identify.

The insidious nature of passive-aggression is that although you may feel the rage underlying your partner's behavior, you can't precisely identify what went wrong or whether it was done on purpose. For example, I've interviewed countless couples who have some room in the house that has gone unfinished for years. Ben and Vicky were one such couple. Vicky would remind (some would say nag) Ben, and he would then partially complete another portion of the task, only to leave it still unfinished. Vicky would then become livid over this repetitive pattern, and she'd say, "You always do this. Why can't you just finish something?" He would sulk, she would feel guilty, and both would shut down.

Vicky could have said, "You always do this *to me!*" which would have been a more accurate reflection of her feelings. She could have said, "I feel like you're telling me how little you care about me," but she grew up with the assumption that she was not good enough, so it's difficult for her to speak this fear out loud.

Vicky sounds as though her only concern is the house, because she's not describing how Ben's negligence affects her. So he turns his back and thinks, "She cares more about this house than about me." This adds to his increasing resentment, which contributes to his lack of interest in completing projects—and so the cycle continues. These two people are not able to address their injuries with each other, so they continue to inflict them. The focus on the house projects diverts their attention from the sense of hurt.

It's likely that Vicky herself can't understand her intense anger over the house projects. In calm moments, she will say to herself, "Maybe I am taking this house business too seriously. I need to lighten up." She then goes home and finds her husband watching

Wheel of Fortune on TV. A towel bar is lying on the floor in front of the unfinished powder room, and for a moment she sees herself slamming the towel bar through his chest. All at once, she's shocked, frightened, and delighted with herself. But the overwhelming fear and self-loathing interrupt and remind her of the hopelessness. She goes to her husband and halfheartedly nags him a little, assuming that there is no hope.

Ben experiences her anger as a lack of caring. He really does believe that she cares more about everyone and everything else than she does about him. He doesn't dare challenge this because history tells him that his worst fears will be confirmed. He expects that if he asks, she'll admit that he is indeed disposable. This is an old fear. He often felt as though his parents didn't really want him around. He protects himself by disengaging, but the hurt remains. He can't understand why she gets so angry just because he watches a little TV. Can he help it if the one show he enjoys happens to be on just when she comes home from work? Is it his fault that the projects around the house never seem to turn out right? People seem never to care about him or like him, but they want so much from him. These people include his boss, his family, and especially his wife. Ben believes that Vicky wishes she were with someone else, and once in a while he feels that it would be a relief to get it over with, to hear from her that she is seeing someone else and that she is leaving him. He thinks to himself, "If you're so unhappy with me, why don't you just leave?" Of course he can't say this except in rare moments of rage.

At first glance, little seems to be going on with Ben and Vicky; in fact, there is far *too much* happening. They're not silent due to lack of stimulus; they're silent because they're overstimulated. They appear numb to each other because they're overaroused by each other and therefore need to retreat to a nearly catatonic state. The combination of early wounds and possible clinical depression make it impossible for them to approach and comfort each other. They cannot ask for more from each other, so they're unable to give to each other.

Evolutionary Tip
Evaluate Your Fighting Style

In a reptilian state, we use many dirty fighting tactics in order to win or escape. Think about your last fight(s) and check off the unfair or destructive tactics you used. Which do you use often?

_____ Name-calling and personal insults

_____ Sarcasm, teasing

_____ Insulting or blaming your partner's family

_____ Lying or telling half-truths

_____ Bringing up history or old stories in order to prove your point

_____ Arguing over insignificant details

_____ Bringing in new topics, such as parenting skills, housework, and the like

_____ Naming experts, books, or friends who support your point

_____ One-upping your partner by listing your own credentials or expertise

_____ Moving toward your partner in an intimidating manner

_____ Threatening to leave, divorce, harm, or vandalize

_____ Forgetting things

_____ Remaining silent

_____ Leaving the scene

These tactics probably seem like good ideas when you use them. Do they still? Have any of them helped you make your point or bring your partner closer?

RECOGNIZING PATTERNS
IN THE CYCLES OF BATTLE

All partners have stories about each other and their lives together. If they're having problems, they see these as linear problems: he did this terrible thing, and I responded thusly; she treated me badly, and I lashed back. This view of the situation can be overwhelming. If you view your problems as a series of daily battles or retreats, you may feel as though you have to work on hundreds of issues. It's more accurate and much more helpful to view marital difficulties as cyclical. A disagreement or battle rarely happens in a vacuum. Something precedes the argument, usually a series of disappointments or negative feelings lead up to the actual disagreement. You might recognize some of the events in such a series immediately, whereas others are almost impossible to identify. For example:

⇒ Mike is late for dinner.

⇒ Sue is angry and frustrated (also tired and hungry) and retaliates angrily.

⇒ Mike counters, and they fight or flee (stop talking).

⇒ Sue feels that her needs are dismissed, and she distances herself from Mike for a period of time.

⇒ Mike feels that all his efforts at work are seen as unimportant, and he sulks resentfully.

⇒ Mike becomes frightened and tries to win Sue back by trying to touch her.

⇒ Sue rejects him but eventually tries to talk to Mike about what has happened.

⇒ Mike rejects talking about the problem for fear of getting into more hot water.

⇒ They reach a kind of truce, and things return to normal.

⇒ Later on, Sue describes Mike as untrustworthy because he is often late.

⇒ Mike complains that Sue doesn't take care of the house, but always criticizes him.

⇒ They both feel disrespected.

⇒ Mike is worried about some bills that have stacked up and feels that he may have to work even more hours to get this under control.

⇒ Sue is worried about those same bills and is annoyed by the idea that Mike blames her.

⇒ Sue ignores Mike when he comes in at the end of the day.

⇒ Mike, annoyed that Sue ignores him, comes home late more often.

You can see that at any point in this cycle, both Sue and Mike can honestly state that the other caused the problem. The magic in looking at cycles is that the couple can see their behaviors as logical and connected, instead of as random acts of aggression. Each negative behavior is in response to some other action or feeling. Looking at patterns, you can see numerous points at which some small change is possible.

The simple diagram here describes much of relationship battle. In this schema, a partner places some demand on the other, who, for whatever reasons, feels overwhelmed or unable to meet the demand. Rather than admit that she feels hurt by her partner's rejection, the asking partner then goes on the attack or withdraws. Rather than admit being overwhelmed and hurt by the attack, the

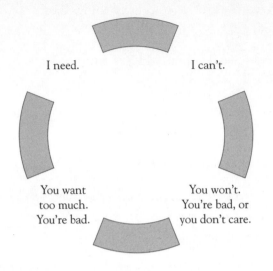

I need.   I can't.

You want   You won't.
too much.   You're bad, or
You're bad.   you don't care.

partner counterattacks. These interactions are totally unfulfilling for both, and the sense of "I need something" remains in both.

Troubled couples often feel overwhelmed by the numerous ways in which they see things not going well in their relationship. You may be able to quickly name twenty different ways in which you offend each other or fail to connect. It seems impossible to solve twenty different problems. But you don't have to fix every single part of the cycle. Instead, you'll discover that as you alter even a tiny piece of this pattern, the rest of the cycle changes as well. For example, if Mike were to limit his possible "late nights" to two or three specific evenings per week, they might agree that these would be quick-and-easy meal nights, or that he was on his own for food. Sue might make nicer meals on those evenings when they have committed to being together for dinner. This does not solve all of their concerns but provides a good-faith effort between them to take the tension out of meals.

These first two chapters have given you an overview of how reptilian responses play a large part in the way we relate and react to each other. Part Two of the book will introduce you to five steps you can take to reduce the reptilian influences that sabotage your relationship and to help you evolve into the kind of loving, caring, respectful partner you've always wanted to be.

Part II

Five Steps to Ending Destructive Fights
and Evolving Toward
More Loving Relationships

3

Step One

Assess Your Relationship

How many therapists does it take to change a
light bulb?
    Only one, but the light bulb really needs to want
to change.

Before you embark on the five steps in this part of the book, please remember this: your relationship is sacred. Never has there been a relationship like yours, and never will there be one like it again. You have to resolve difficulties and develop your intimacy in ways that are appropriate to the two complex individuals you are. That makes it difficult to construct a one-size-fits-all, step-by-step program that can work for everyone.

So as you read on through the next several chapters and the five steps to ending stupid fighting, keep in mind that because your relationship is like no one else's, you may need only two steps, or you may need to repeat step four . . . sixteen times. Or you may find that one of the steps I suggest inspired you to think of a slightly different step that would work better for you. And don't be concerned if you're unable to accomplish your relationship goals in five steps, or if one of those steps should fail miserably for you. Realize that as you cycle through these steps, you can select the practices that are most useful to you and your partner.

I mentioned this in the Introduction but it is so important I am going to say it again. Everything you do in working on your relationship is merely an experiment. If you do not achieve what you consider acceptable improvement in your relationship after completing any or all of the five steps in this book, it doesn't mean that your relationship is doomed or that your partner doesn't care enough. It means that the particular process you tried was not right for you at this time, and it's time for a new experiment! Part of your success as a couple will depend on giving each other a little more room to make errors and to try things that don't work. Such acceptance of one another's efforts also allows you to take more risks with each other. This adventurousness will increase your sense of intimacy.

LET THE EVOLUTION BEGIN

When things are not going well, a common reptilian response is to blame someone else:[1] "I only do this because he does that!" "I wouldn't have to be this way if she wasn't so . . . !" We feel better about ourselves (and can justify our own bad behavior) when we know we are the person who is right and, at the same time, the person who is wronged.

You can keep insisting that all the difficulties in your relationship are your partner's fault, but this will never produce positive results. The truth is that all successful attempts at relationship change involve personal responsibility and individual change. The only behaviors, thoughts, and reactions you can change or control, however, are your own.

Problems arise when people take responsibility for each other—for instance, when they assume that a complaint means that they're expected to mend something. This can seem totally unfair when they're not sure what's broken. Are they supposed to guess? The resulting hopelessness and helplessness will predictably turn to hurt, panic, and rage, all because they assumed that they were supposed to *fix* their partner or their partner's situation.

The thought that they should take *less* responsibility for changing each other is one of the most difficult concepts for couples to grasp. Aren't you supposed to care about each other and try to help each other? Isn't it a part of your love that you want your partner to be happy and content? Of course it is, but you cannot and need not change or fix your loved one. The difference is huge, and ignoring the difference can result in feelings of helplessness, hurt, and betrayal, for both of you.

Some people actually try so hard to fix the other person that it becomes cloying and annoying: "Can I get you anything?" "No thanks." "A drink? A sandwich? An aspirin?" "No thanks." "How about some chicken soup? Or a nice hot toddy?" "NO THANKS!"

Instead of being helpful, this concern comes across as intrusive and disrespectful, and makes the "helpee" want to scream, "Stop telling me what I'm thinking and what I need!" To the Reptilian Brain, these acts of intended kindness can be perceived as assaults and therefore bring about a combative response.

To avoid such a response and to change not your partner (which is impossible) but your relationship, focus on yourself. You are the only one you can change and in this step the focus is on you. The assessments in this chapter will help you get to know yourself, and your reptilian drives, better.[2]

PERSONAL ASSESSMENTS

As the first step in taking less responsibility for your partner, you are going to step back and observe. Don't try to change anything. Begin by exploring your own stress level and trigger points. Before describing the changes you need in your relationship, do a quick inventory of yourself. Grab some paper or a notebook and make some notes on the following self-assessments. I encourage you to first do this by yourself. If you and your partner are reading this book together, you should still keep your answers private at this time.[3] You can decide later how you want to discuss your answers. Just wait until it feels safe to reveal the information. Hang on to these notes. You'll want to review them later, and I hope you'll want to share them with your partner.

These assessments help you identify aspects of yourself or your behavior that may be harming your relationship or your ability to work on your relationship. They also help you recognize some of the ways in which you and your partner have deviated from behaviors and agreements that once worked for you. As you begin to see the wide variety of pressures on your relationship, you'll find that you and your partner are less blaming of one another and less likely to think about problems in a one-dimensional, look-what-you-do-to-me way.

Self-Assessment 1: Your Health and Welfare

When you're attempting to make any life change, it's useful to conduct an inventory of how you're doing in all areas of your life. It may point out areas in which you will have to be extra careful or give yourself extra time, space, or credit.

- Health:[4] Do you have any pain or medical problems that affect your mood or thinking? Be detailed here; you should list—headaches, back pain, gastric problems, or any other health issues.

- External stressors: How do your job, family members, friends, or other pressures affect your relationship?

- Mental health:[5] Do you have any possible symptoms of depression or anxiety?

- Chemical use or other addictive behaviors: Do you tend to have most arguments with your partner when one of you has been drinking or taking drugs? Do you have a dependency problem with gambling, shopping, exercising, or other behavior that intrudes on your relationship?

- Stress management skills:[6] How are you handling stress right now? What methods do you use to bring down your own stress level?

- Social supports: Who is in your corner? Which relationships do you feel really good about? Are any of those supports in fact negative toward your relationship?

- Financial worries: Are you in any personal debt?

- Sexual interest and performance: Have there been any changes recently? To what have you attributed these changes?

In asking yourself these questions, you might want to make special note of any factor that may be playing a role in some repetitive problem you have with your partner. This is an opportunity, away from the field of battle, to review your own strengths and weaknesses. For example, if your partner says that you don't seem interested in him anymore, this review may alert you to a personal issue that is not related to him. For instance, if you've been under a lot of stress at work and aren't sleeping very well, you may not have much interest in sex. In this regard, your partner's perception that you are less interested in him is accurate—but not because of him. If you discuss with him that you are stressed out, not sleeping, and feeling like you can't get very aroused, the two of you might be able to problem-solve around those issues. If you don't talk about your situation, your partner's perception that you're no longer interested will harm your relationship.

Self-Assessment 2: How Do You Respond to Stress?

Some mornings it just doesn't seem worth it to gnaw through the leather straps.

Emo Philips

Reptilian Brain responses often jump to the forefront in times of stress. Review the following list of symptoms and check off the ones you tend to experience in your body and thoughts during stressful times (including during disagreements with your partner):

☐ Changes in sleep—both insomnia and hypersomnia (excessive sleep)

☐ Changes in appetite—either an increase or decrease

☐ Irritability, anger outbursts, tantrums

☐ Jumpiness, feeling nervous and on edge

☐ Mood swings—happy to sad to angry, and so on

☐ Muscle pain—headaches, neck or back pain, stiffness

☐ Gastric upset—stomachaches, heartburn

☐ Decreased concentration and short-term memory

☐ Increased number of illnesses

☐ Withdrawal and isolation

☐ Tearfulness

☐ Increased addictive behavior—including alcohol, drug, nicotine, or caffeine use; shopping, eating, sex, gambling, or exercising

☐ Decreased libido—performance problems, decreased interest in sex[7]

☐ Vulnerability, suspicion, paranoia[8]

☐ Any other symptoms that seem to fit your experience

As you look over your symptoms, notice how they relate to each other. When feeling irritable, on edge, and vulnerable, you're unlikely to be able to relax and enjoy closeness, touch, or sexual intercourse. Lack of sleep creates physical and cognitive difficulties, including suspiciousness. Stress can lead to insomnia, which creates the cognitive and social problems of irritability, vulnerability, and paranoia. Clearly a period of prolonged sleep deprivation would be a poor time to work on your relationship. Edgy, irritable, confused, and suspicious may not be the best state in which to approach your love life. You can't always choose when to talk with your partner, but when you're struggling with pain, insomnia, or other impairment, it's essential that you keep your goals realistic. Focus on solving immediate, well-defined problems and save the broader challenges for a better time.

Evolutionary Tip
How to Lower Tension

Here are some quick stress-reduction techniques you can use when facing a difficult situation with your partner:

1. Take a long, deep breath, expanding first your abdomen and then your chest, and finally raising your shoulders. This "abdominal breath" will stretch the chest muscles, slow your heart rate, and rush oxygen into your bloodstream and so to your brain.

2. Take a hot shower. Warmth relaxes muscle tension and aids in blood flow.

3. Do a brief focusing exercise. For instance, sit still and identify one thing through each of your five senses. Ask yourself, "What am I seeing? What am I hearing? What am I touching or feeling? What do I taste? What do I smell?" Notice that these do not require any interpretation or deep thought.

(continued on next page)

Evolutionary Tip
How to Lower Tension (continued)

4. Do some stretching. Tension often sits in the back of the neck and lower back, and some brief stretching can help relieve it. This little "time-out" may also help slow down the argument and get you back in touch with yourself and your goals.

5. Make some notes. The stressed-out brain does not organize. Writing engages more brain functions and forces you to organize your thoughts. It will cut down on the wheel-spinning thinking prevalent in stressed-out people.

6. Work a crossword puzzle or perform some other diverting task. Because of the higher-level thinking required to solve them, puzzles also help you be more creative and analytical.

Self-Assessment 3: Relationship Concerns

> One morning, a rather disgruntled-looking wife said to her husband, "You know the Petersons next door?"
>
> "Of course I do," he replied. "Nice folks."
>
> "Well," she said, "every morning he gives her a big hug and a kiss before he goes to work. Why don't you do that?"
>
> "I'd be glad to," he answered, "but I hardly know her that well."

What do you see as your current relationship problems? Write out your answers to the questions that follow; be as specific as possible. These details will aid your work in later chapters.

- What are the most frequent disagreements between you and your partner?

- Are you more likely to fight or flee?

- When are you most likely to fight or avoid each other?

- What is your usual way of shutting your partner down?

- What is his or her usual response to your shut-down method?

- What was the best time you have had recently with your partner?

- Describe a difficult discussion you had with your partner that ended in a positive resolution.

- What do you feel you need in order for you to treat your partner well? Does she do anything specific that actually prevents you from wanting to be close to her?

- What prevents you from asking for things you need from your partner?

- How do you attempt to get positive attention from your partner?

- What do you do that gets negative attention, such as frustration, anger, or silence, from your partner?

- What is your partner asking for that you do not want to give?

- What is your partner asking for that you don't believe you *can* give even if you wanted to?

- How often do you display anger in a way that upsets your partner? Is anger a problem for you in other areas of your life?[9]

- What do you do that really drives your partner crazy? (Come on—admit it!)

This self-assessment is to encourage you to think about how difficulties unfold in your relationship, and the role you play in them. Most of the questions don't allow you to focus on your partner's misdeeds. The goal at this stage is to be clear about what *you* bring to the table.

FAMILY ASSESSMENTS

Nothing is fun for the whole family.

Jerry Seinfeld

Your family forms you in subtle and profound ways. The late Carl Whittaker, a famous family therapist, is quoted as saying that "marriage is the process of two tribes exchanging hostages." In order to understand the reptilian defenses in your fearful and hostile interactions, you must understand the tribal rituals and traditions through which you have developed. Partners can be incredibly helpful to each other in understanding themselves and their families when they discuss these matters in respectful ways.

What You Can Learn from Family Structure

The first clues to what you have learned from your family and therefore bring to the relationship lie in the structure of the family. Everything about your family structure has meaning. The roles of each of the individuals, the age at which special or harmful events took place, your position in the birth order—all provide information about who you are.[10]

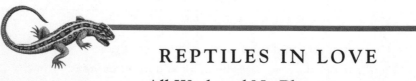

REPTILES IN LOVE
All Work and No Play

Lyle and Kate came to see me with a laundry list of marital complaints. Lyle described Kate as being a nag, always on him about something and never wanting to have any fun. Kate described Lyle as unpredictable and undependable. She noted that every time they were to meet, Lyle was late. When they agreed to save money, Lyle spent more. She said that Lyle didn't want to grow up. He wasn't motivated to get promotions or go back to school, and it seemed as though whenever there were plans to be made or bills to be paid, she ended up being the responsible one.

Lyle said that he felt as though he didn't have any freedom at all. He grieved the fact that he and Kate used to have a lot of fun together and painted the town red. Now she always wanted to stay in, and she accused him of spending the night with other women whenever he came in late. She scrutinized any purchase he made and wanted to know where every dime went. They had tried to write up a budget once, but fought so bitterly that they almost ended up calling the police on each other.

Kate acknowledged that they used to have a lot of fun together. That ended for her when she became pregnant. They got married and were both very serious about wanting to spend their lives together and having a family. Telling me this, Kate tearfully complained that it was as if she had two children. Lyle reddened at this and looked ready to leave the room. He said that he'd heard this before and hated it when she talked to him like this. "Then stop acting like a child," she replied.

Kate and Lyle are caught in a classic bind: they married their opposites. To understand this we must first understand their roles in their families. Kate was the eldest of four siblings. Her parents had worked outside the home in blue-collar jobs since Kate was around eight years old, and she had taken over most of the child-care responsibilities by the time she was eleven. Neither of her parents made a lot of money, and the family had to scrimp to get by. Her dad was a reliable worker but liked a good time. He was a lot of fun (especially when he drank). Her parents frequently argued about his spending and drinking.

Lyle was the youngest of three, and he was always "a good kid" according to his family. His older sister took care of him because both their parents worked. His mother and father were always fighting and seemed constantly on the edge of breaking up.

Lyle was attracted to Kate like a tornado to a trailer park. She was pretty and neat. She appreciated a good laugh and enjoyed his ideas and schemes. Kate went for Lyle too. He was funny and could always think of things to do. Lyle could make anything seem like a joke. Sure she saw some warning signs, but what the hell!

Kate didn't realize that part of what she saw in Lyle was her good-timing father, whom she loved and defended desperately. She had never laughed as she did with Lyle. Lyle saw the calming effect that Kate had on him. When he was with her, the chaos of his upbringing seemed "a million miles away." He didn't realize that sometimes he thought of her as his older sister.

They were trapped.

The very positives they needed from each other became the irritants. The more Kate tried to straighten Lyle out, the more he resisted and acted "like a kid." The more he ignored or avoided her, the more he screwed up, the more she chased him and argued with him. The more desperate each became to be treated with respect, the more they were forced into their roles, which were becoming less and less helpful and appreciated.

Once they recognized the roles they were playing, they were able to move gently back toward center with each other. Lyle took on more responsibilities around the house. Kate needed to avoid talking down to Lyle as if he were her child. Kate still worried about things a bit more than Lyle; he tended to be more playful and silly than she. But once they viewed their behavior in the context of their family roles and began to help each other with the strengths and weaknesses of the respective roles, they redeveloped their intimacy. They could view each other as fuller, more complex individuals than just the roles they had fallen into.

The assessment exercises that follow will help you flesh out your understanding of what you have learned from your respective families and cultures.

Family Assessment 1: Family History

You may develop some interesting ideas about your thoughts, emotions, and behaviors with your partner as you think about your family's history. As stated earlier, I hope you will eventually deepen your intimacy with your partner by exploring your family histories together.

- Were your parents married? Did they remain married?

- If they separated or divorced, how old were you when that happened?

- If they divorced, did they remarry? Are there half siblings or stepsiblings?

- What relationship did you have with these "step-others"?

- How many siblings do you have? What is your position in the birth order?

- Were you or any of your siblings adopted? If so, at what age(s)?

- Who lived in your house while you were growing up?

- In what kind of house, houses, or apartments did you grow up? How big? How many rooms? Where did family members spend most of their time? What places do you associate with each person?

- How old were you and your parents at key events? How old were they at the time you and each of your siblings were born?

- If there were any big changes or tragedies, how did they fit into your life span and that of your family?

Family Assessments 2 and 3: Rituals and Traditions (Yours and Your Partner's)

It's the hidden or subtle rituals and traditions in our childhood that form our future. We learn most of what we know about human interactions, about men and women, about authority figures and groups, when we are quite young.

If you grow up in a family in which loud voices lead to someone getting hurt, for example, you're likely to respond to loud voices with fear. This is a learned response. It doesn't matter whether there is an actual physical or emotional attack; your body will be sending off alarms that you won't be able to ignore. You'll most likely respond in a style that reflects your earliest learned coping mechanisms. If it was your usual style to withdraw and hide in your room when voices were raised or someone was getting hurt, then it's very likely that you'll want to withdraw and hide from the source of loudness in your current situation. If your partner grew up in a family where raised voices were merely statements of passion and excitement, she will be totally astonished and hurt that you run away from her when she raises her voice.

The list of questions about rituals and traditions that follows is not exhaustive, so you might want to add any additional ways to describe your family's culture. As you make notes in response to this list, what do you feel? What questions elicit a bit of happiness, pride, anger, or sadness in you? These may give you some clues about areas of hurt in your current relationship.

- When did your family eat meals? What were the dietary traditions in the family?

- How were special events and holidays celebrated?

- How was your birthday celebrated?

- How did family members deal with disappointments or loss?

- How did you get attention?

- How did family members work out disagreements?

- How did your parents or other family members demon-strate affection to each other?

- How did your parents show affection to you and to your siblings? How did you and your siblings demonstrate affection?

- Could affection ever be dangerous or painful?

- Who were on what teams in the family? (Did males gang up on females? Did mother and son sometimes exclude the father? Did father talk about marital issues with one of the children? Were there other special relationships?)

- What were the best times in the family, and what were the worst?

- What jobs did family members hold outside the home?

- Who did what chores in the home?

- What were the spiritual views in the family? Was there agreement or dissension?

- What were the political traditions in the family? Was there agreement or dissension?

- Who was admired in the family? Who was definitely not admired? Did you feel the same way about those admired or disdained persons, and have your feelings changed?

When you're done, go through the same list of questions and make some notes on what you understand about your partner's family. What have you learned so far? Which questions would you expect to elicit some strong reactions from your partner? How do these match up with areas that brought up questions or strong feelings for you?

Family Assessment 4: Interfamily Relationships

Now let's talk about how you and your partner deal with each other's families. Write down your answers to the following questions:

- Whom do you like in your partner's family? Whom do you not like in your partner's family?

- Who seems to like you in your partner's family? Who in your partner's family doesn't seem to like you?

- What do you know about your partner's family history?

- What about your partner's family makes you curious or puzzled?

- What is the most interesting story you know about your partner's family?

- Whom does your partner like in your family? Whom in your family does your partner not like?

- Who in your family seems to like your partner? Who in your family doesn't seem to like your partner?

- What about your family confuses your partner?

- What embarrasses you about your family? How does your partner handle this?

- What secrets about your family have you kept? (I don't necessarily believe that all of a family's secrets must be disclosed. Such secrets need to be addressed cautiously and with respect.)

- How do you and your partner handle discussions about your family?

- Which family discussions seem to go well, and which become heated? Why?

- What does your partner want from you regarding his or her family that you find difficult to offer? What gets in the way?

- Have you or your partner learned any very powerful negative lessons from your families or been traumatized in some way that makes closeness or trust difficult for either of you?

Family Assessment 5: Sharing Family Information

In almost every initial couples session, one of the partners will want to explain to me that their partner's negative, nasty, nearly criminal behavior is due to his or her upbringing. Needless to say, this is neither helpful nor well received by the partner.

Most of us have theories about why our partner acts a certain way. It's not that these theories are wrong; it's often helpful to understand the origin of your partner's behavior. It's just that these theories are not useful when your partner perceives them as just another criticism or attack. So when you're fighting, never try to convince your partner that his transgressions or failings in life are due to bad parenting or sick family members. He will *always* oppose you. He simply must.

Now, to the degree that you feel comfortable, go over the previous four assessments with your partner. You need not review every single item or reveal anything you're not comfortable revealing as yet. Remember, we're approaching this process slowly and with caution, and you may be able to reveal these things to each other when you finish this book . . . or in a month . . . or in a year. That's something to which you can look forward with great anticipation. After talking about the assessments, think about these questions:

- Did you discover anything new from sharing these assessments with your partner?

- When there were surprises, how did you discuss these, and how did you interpret not knowing these things?

- Did you recognize any of your own issues in your family background or see how your upbringing influenced your current problems?

- Did you gain any information that will help you better appreciate or understand your partner?

- Did you gain any information that will help you better appreciate or understand your partner's family?

- Did you learn anything that makes it easier for you to offer something your partner has needed of you, with respect to his or her family?

Evolutionary Tip
Gather Information Playfully

The assessments in this and other chapters are not made up of researched, scientifically correct questions. Many of them are, however, questions that I typically ask in therapy and that help me get to know a person. Invent your own questions and opportunities for exploring your partner and his or her culture as if you were an anthropologist studying a strange new tribe. This will help you move from being frightened, angry, or disengaged to being curious. Here are some ideas:

Where were you when . . . ? **The rest of this question may depend on your age, in terms of a critical event that formed** a part of your understanding of the world. (I remember seeing my mother cry over a murdered president when I came home from school. I remember the whole family watching it on TV when astronauts first landed on the moon.)

How did you find out the truth about Santa Claus? (**Probably my older brothers . . . the bastards!**)

To whom were you first sexually attracted? (**Betty Rubble, Elizabeth Montgomery in** *Bewitched,* **or Laura Petrie. I never could commit.**)

Who was the most peculiar teacher you had in school? (**I won't name her in print. She tried awfully hard, and in retrospect I'm not sure how she kept from strangling me.**)

Taking yourselves less seriously and allowing play back into the relationship will permit you to get closer to each other. Such playful exploration may also place some useful distance between your intimate relationship and your relationship with your families of origin. Many couples are surprised to find that once they create this separation, their relationship with each other's families is much improved, and the family of origin has been removed as a target in their battles with each other.

UNDERSTANDING YOUR PSYCHOLOGICAL CONTRACT

The psychological contract consists of the expectations—realistic or not—held by two people who have decided to be together.[11] The majority of this contract is never discussed out loud by the two lovers, mostly because of the huge number of conscious and unconscious assumptions involved. Lovers who are becoming committed partners do usually discuss the large, apparent issues, but even on those they may gloss over things that are truly important. They hold the hidden expectation that "if my partner really loves me, he or she will gladly adapt in this area to please me, and then I will be even more certain he or she really loves me." The frightening unspoken assumption here is that "if my partner does not understand my needs and meet my expectations, it means that he or she doesn't really love me, or at least not as much as I had thought." Devastating in its simplicity, isn't it?

Some battles may be about clearly identifiable breaches of contract. In such cases, both partners are aware that there is a disagreement about how they treat each other. Many elements of the contract, however, are difficult to identify. The subjects over which a couple choose to fight may have very little to do with their actual disappointments. Many battles are therefore recurrent and never resolved, and they leave both partners confused and frustrated.

Simply put, couples fight the wrong battles. They fight about topics that are substitutes for much more critical issues they wish to avoid or don't recognize. Consider a recent disagreement with your partner. Were you clear and targeted as to what you needed? If you were wondering if your partner was bored with you, but you ended up arguing about not going out enough, you should imagine a huge game show buzzer going off. "Sorry," the game show host would say. "Thank you for playing, but you're completely on the wrong subject. The winning category was 'Do you enjoy being with me?' for six thousand points, and instead you chose 'You're too lazy to go out dancing,' for ten measly points. You lose. You can come back next week and play again, but for God's sake, try to shape up."

Here are more examples of unspoken psychological contracts:

> When we were dating, you hung on every word I said. You seemed so interested. Therefore, my psychological contract with you is that you will always be interested in what I have

to say, and any failure to do so will be perceived as a rejection of me and of our love.

When we were dating, it seemed as if you couldn't wait to be alone with me and get your clothes off. My psychological contract with you is that you will always, regardless of work, kids, illness, or anger, be prepared at a moment's notice to have sex. With an expectation of this latter sort one might then think, "now you seem to act as though sex is a chore, so the contract is broken. It lets me know that you weren't really in love with me. If we don't have agreement in this critical area our love cannot be real."

If you're carrying around one of these psychological contracts or a similar one, you may know in your most rational state that your expectation is not realistic. This realization doesn't lessen the hurt, but it does prevent you from voicing your feelings to your partner. Instead, you may find yourself saying, "You never listen to me" or "You never want to have sex. What's wrong with you?" This language increases injury and prevents you and your partner from actively discussing the changes needed or the disappointments you are experiencing.

Our contracts with our intimate partners develop from needs and assumptions that are based on our circumstances, family backgrounds, values, and previous dating experiences, along with fantasies we have created from love stories, fairy tales, the media, or pornography. These expectations permeate every aspect of our lives together and are often not discussed at all. Most people can't really step outside themselves enough to say, "Wait a minute. This is a tradition in my family, and it's something I always expect to happen. It's as natural to me as breathing, yet it may not be a part of my partner's experience at all."

What do you see as your assumptions about the following contract elements? Do you think your partner holds these same or similar assumptions? Does she know about these contract elements and would she approve of them?

- How tidy does the house need to be?

- Who does which chores?

- Who gets up early and makes coffee?

- What types of humor are seen as funny?

- When, where, and how is it okay or best to touch each other?

- Who's responsible for what kinds of child care?

- How often is "I love you" supposed to be said?

- Who pays what bills, and in what financial situations is the partner consulted?

- Which friends are okay?

- Are there any limitations on friendships with others?

- How much time should we spend together?

- How much time can we spend apart?

- What is "quality time" for us?

- What is an acceptable way to dress?

- Who spends too much? (Have we ever defined what "too much" means?)

- What are the rituals for going to bed at night?

- Who has the "final word" on which issues?

- When is it okay to critique a partner's appearance or behavior?

- On what subjects can we joke?

- When is sarcasm humorous, and when is it hurtful?

You can probably add a bunch of items to this already lengthy list. As you review the list, think about how you developed your views on each item. Now think about how your partner may have developed his or her views on the same item. Are you very likely to see this topic similarly given the different sources of information you bring to your current relationship?

Let's take sarcasm, for instance. I grew up with four brothers, and the competition was extraordinary. Sarcasm, name-calling, and pranks were daily occurrences. My wife also comes from a large family but is much less used to such witty verbal repartee. She comes to a discussion with a different set of expectations. She has a great sense of humor and considerable tolerance, but nevertheless may not always appreciate some of my commentary on serious subjects. Also, because use of sarcasm was an early learned behavior for me, I'm more likely to be sarcastic when some perceived threat activates my Reptilian Brain.

Changes in the Psychological Contract

The psychological contract in any relationship is subject to constant change and revision. It's not necessarily a breach of contract if a person's expectations for his or her lover change over time. Such changes are actually necessary. The test is whether a couple can incorporate the change into their relationship without feeling frightened or betrayed. We know that people approach transitions in vastly different ways and are often quite uncomfortable with even small changes. Yet the nature of life is that it's filled with changes. Financial circumstances, jobs, health, family relationships, and living conditions—all are prone to changes that can be dramatic and sweeping.

When contracts change drastically, it's common to experience all the physiological, emotional, and cognitive responses to stress described in Chapter One. The couple must adjust to a whole new reality about their relationship, and this is fraught with danger because of all the deficits we discussed earlier that characterize the thinking of a person under severe stress—such deficits as memory problems, lack of empathy, difficulty with creative thought and abstract reasoning, damaged organizational skills, and increased suspiciousness and irritability, just to name a few.

There are two main types of change that seriously affect relationships:

- *Change due to external forces:* Any couple faced with a change in their contract—a crisis in their relationship—may well find themselves treating each other poorly, even if the contract has been breached due to outside forces, not due to anything that either of them has done wrong (for example, when one partner suddenly has to work the night shift or when one of them has to spend a large amount of time caring for an ailing parent). The couple may find themselves tired, disorganized, and disappointed, and furthermore find that whenever they do see each other, there is all the mundane stuff of running a house to talk about. They really have very little time for anything fun or imaginative and are always trying to catch up on the business of living.

- *Change initiated by one of the partners:* What about changes in the contract that are sought by one of the partners, which both partners recognize as a redrafting of their original agreements? For example, a partner who originally described herself as a homebody decides that she wants to go out more often and maybe even travel. "She took a damn college course, and now she thinks she's Amelia Earhart." When a partner changes the contract because of newly perceived needs, this can feel like a bait and switch. Or as in a cartoon I once saw, in which a woman is saying to her husband, "It seems like everything I liked about you was a limited time, introductory offer." Can you picture aspects of your psychological contract that your partner might not know about, or with which he or she would not agree? Try to keep this in mind as you proceed. We'll revisit this concept in Chapter Eight when discussing betrayals. Perhaps it will be helpful for you to think about how you developed your ideas about relationships and the stories that you have about yourself, your partner, and your relationship.

UNDERSTANDING THE MYTHS OF YOUR RELATIONSHIP

Two guys were talking at their coffee break, delving into science and philosophy as usual. One asked, "You ever heard of Freudian slips?"

The other replied, "If you mean those times when you say something similar to what you meant to say but with a slight change that reveals a different subconscious meaning, then yes I do. In fact, it happened to me just this morning at breakfast. I meant to ask my wife to pass the toast, and instead I said, 'You bitch, you've ruined my life!'"

I have one more individual assessment for you. Now that you've examined your health, stress level, coping mechanisms, and family background, it's time to look at the stories you have developed about your relationship.[12] Initially these stories are predominantly positive, and they establish the positive aspects of our relationships. Our interpretations of our environment are fallible, however. We make mistakes because we experience the world through our personal filters. These filters are composed of our history, culture, needs, family background, emotional health, religion, and numerous other factors. We see a new lover through these same filters. We initially ignore the negatives and exaggerate the positives. We create a story that feels right and defines this idealized person as meeting most or all of our needs. The story does not allow for much objective analysis if we're deciding that this is a person with whom we want to dedicate ourselves permanently. In fact, the intoxication of romantic love includes biological changes that render such critical analysis virtually impossible.

Think for a moment of some of these romantic stories. They are the "happily ever after" stories that we have dreamed about since we were children.

> She's beautiful. I'll always be amazed and surprised by her grace and beauty.

> He's warm and funny all the time. He'll always be easygoing and warm. Unlike others, he would forgive me anything and only love me more when I make little mistakes.

> We are the perfect couple. We won't fight because we agree on everything.

> She's her own person, and her self-confidence and talent inspire me.

As reality smacks us soundly upside our head, the stories may become less positive and more restrictive. Have you noticed yourself describing your partner in more and more fixed, robotic terms?

> He never does anything around the house.

> She never wants to do anything fun.

> He never spends any time with the children.

> She's always talking to her mother but won't talk to me at all.

> All he ever wants me for is sex.

Unfortunately, the longer these stories go unchallenged, the more the negative traits have a way of becoming expected from each other. Both partners truly do find themselves living like robots. They remain in a rut of negative expectations from which there is no escape. They don't trust each other to participate in change, and they're unwilling to expose themselves to further disappointment and hurt. Many of our stories involve needing to be treated fairly, so equal participation in the attempts to change seems to be extremely important to us.

The following list demonstrates the way initial "sainthood stories" (all positive) become betrayal stories. Do you recognize any of your patterns here? Add any stories that you can think of now that may limit you in perceiving your partner and your relationship accurately.

Saintly Story	*Betrayal Story*
He's so funny.	He never misses a chance to insult and humiliate me.
She's so lively and energetic.	She'll flirt with anyone male.
He respects his parents.	He chooses his mother over me and can't seem to leave home.
She's so organized and efficient.	She's controlling every aspect of my life.
He's good with money and will be an excellent provider.	He could make a nickel cry, and I'm tired of needing to defend every cent I spend.
She's smart, and I love to hear her talk.	She talks all the time, and I can never win. She outtalks me every time.
He's playful.	He's immature.
She likes my simple interests.	She thinks I'm stupid and backward.
He supports my needs.	He never has an idea of his own.
She knows what she wants.	She doesn't care what I want.
He's ambitious.	He's married to his job. He doesn't care about the kids and me.

Saintly Story	*Betrayal Story*
She loves the kids and is a great mom.	She loves the kids so much she has no time for me.
He knows how to have a good time.	He won't do anything for me or around the house. He's always out with his friends.
We have a great sex life.	All he thinks about is sex. He's just using me.

Throughout the rest of this book you are going to be encouraged to abandon these limiting stories and to become more curious about your partner and all the possibilities for closeness, playfulness, and intimacy that now await you and your partner.

———————

To make progress on your relationship, you must first be prepared to assess yourself. Looking at your physical and mental advantages and disadvantages allows you to objectively examine areas of tension that are affecting your relationship. Understanding your family heritage and culture and those of your partner is essential to a loving relationship. When we analyze our various relationships with others, we're really examining ourselves, and we're naturally self-protective. With a trusted partner, however, you may fearlessly explore your roles and the impact that family and friends have on you. This process will deepen your understanding of yourself as well as of your partner. You'll find that sharing the information from these assessments has brought you closer to your partner. You are now on the same team. Information is one thing—what you do with it is another thing altogether. I hope that this chapter has helped you get a better handle on what you want and need from your relationship. In the next chapter, you'll learn how to safely convey that information to your partner.

4

Step Two

Learn to Communicate in a Nonreptilian Manner

*A couple had finally achieved their dream of buying a
small horse ranch in Wyoming. A close friend flew in
to visit them and see how the ranch was coming. As
they looked over the spread, the friend asked, "Well,
what did you name your ranch?"*

*The husband responded, "You know we can never
agree on anything, and we just couldn't come up with
a name that appealed to both of us. We finally called
it the Fortune Smiles Rocking Horse Whispering
Pines Lazy R Mountain Overlook Ranch."*

*"Wow," the friend exclaimed, "that's really quite
a name. But where are your horses?"*

*"None of 'em survived the branding," his buddy
responded sadly.*

Remember that famous line from *Cool Hand Luke:* "What we
have here is a failure to communicate"? That could be the
mantra of 95 percent of the couples who come to me for therapy.
For some, the problem is that one or both of the partners don't want
to communicate. For most, however, the problem is that they just
don't know how to do it without getting that old Reptilian Brain
all riled up and ready to defend itself.

In this chapter, you'll find a number of strategies that will help you create a sense of safety in your relationship. Remember that each of these is a proposed experiment for you and your partner. These experiments are not designed to answer any specific marital problem; instead they're designed to help you soothe yourselves, reengage your higher brain capacities, and reconnect so that you're able to solve marital problems, in any category, no matter how daunting. Keep your assessments from Chapter Three handy; these will remind you to focus on yourself instead of on your partner.

By now you're aware of the reptilian basis of the problems in communication. You agree, I hope, that in order to improve relationships and particularly to resolve differences, it's necessary to lower the intensity before tackling overwhelming problems. Let's assume, then, that basically you would like to communicate with your partner. You'd like her to listen to you and even sometimes agree with you. You'd like her to do well and prosper and to feel good about herself and, therefore, be able to treat you well. When she turns away from you or seems to ignore you, it makes you a little crazy. You don't want to yell at her or insult her. You "just wish she'd listen, damn it!"

How can you get her to do that?

You can't.

However, it's been my experience that when couples are able to structure a businesslike meeting around difficult topics, with time limits, limitation of side subjects, and avoidance of personal attacks, they're often able to accomplish positive work very quickly. And, unlike the horse ranchers in the joke, they lose nothing of value.

PLANNING AND ORGANIZING A PARTNERSHIP MEETING

In the Introduction to this book, I explained that I do not take a romantic approach in my work. My initial goal is to reduce the intensity and fear that keep a couple separated, distant, or angry. I don't try to push for intimacy before such arousing and potentially disabling feelings have been resolved (or are at least on their way to being resolved).

So I prefer to take a businesslike approach and work toward partnership first: a businesslike relationship emphasizing trust and safety. When partners have reduced the tension and level of threat, they can respect each other's differences and function at their best.

Unfortunately, many couples who come to see me have gotten to the point where some of their most difficult or hurtful discussions feel like guerrilla warfare. Has this ever happened to you? You are settling down for the evening, exhausted from your day; your mind's on all kinds of things, and you just want to go blank in front of your favorite television show. Suddenly you're ambushed by your partner with a question, phrase, comment, or request that you really didn't see coming. You hear, "we need to talk." The lights seem to dim, you hear haunting music in the background, and your body tenses, preparing for battle or flight. He or she notes your immediate surprise and irritation, and—bang—you are in a firefight.

People frequently bring up difficult subjects spontaneously, taking their partners completely off guard. The initiator struggles with an issue all day and decides to do something about it. The receiver is unprepared and responds in a defensive manner. The initiator is then hurt and angry that his or her partner doesn't want to help solve the problem. Both partners are quickly reptilian; in fact, they're so aware of each other that they can start the battle with just a look, a gesture, or a sigh. Often it's the surprise that causes the reptilian response, not necessarily the difficult subject.[1]

I encourage couples to schedule business meetings (which I call partnership meetings) in order to take care of specific troublesome topics. Understand that in my language, "business" can mean any negotiated event or issue between the couple. This may mean financial issues or household chores, or it may mean such hot items as parenting concerns, sexuality, or an issue related to one of the partner's families. As you master these brief meetings, you'll undoubtedly make more progress in a half hour than you did in the days, weeks, months, or years in which you have approached and avoided these topics and frustrated one another.

It's neither possible nor necessary to *always* schedule such discussions, but scheduled meetings can be very helpful. This is akin to any other business meeting: the degree to which the partners are able to stay clear and focused on a specific subject is the degree to which the meeting will be successful. Businesslike partnership meetings have several advantages:

- The surprise factor will be gone, thus reducing reptilian knee-jerk self-protection.

- You know what's on the agenda, you can do your homework, and you can make some notes on what you hope to accomplish.

- In preparation for the meeting, you can provide each other with any necessary information or ideas to help facilitate the meeting agenda.

- This structure will reduce the likelihood of being distracted into "red herring" discussions or random battles.

Remember, the Reptilian Brain is by definition disorganized. When reptilian, you will always be tempted to bring into the discussion lots of peripheral or circumstantial issues.[2] Here are several steps you can take to make it easier to remain calm and businesslike:

1. **Set the time and place.** In setting the stage for effective communication, give careful consideration to all the seemingly mundane aspects of effective meeting planning. Consider at what times both of you are best able to communicate. When are the kids not

around? Is one of you a night owl and the other a morning person? Is it best then to meet for lunch or in the afternoon for coffee, in order to discuss business?

Where should you meet? The bedroom is for rest and physical intimacy, and I discourage using it for these meetings. Often sitting at a dining room or kitchen table with notepads in front of you is optimal. Remember that this is like a business meeting. You want to accomplish what is on the agenda.

2. **Take notes.** Most couples find it very difficult to stay on one subject when they are experiencing stress. They begin to plan a vacation, and suddenly one of them says, "We can't take a vacation because you spend too much money." This sounds like a comment on vacation but is really a different subject. One way to handle these situations is for the partners to draw two columns in their notepads and say that the money issue is important but is in column B. Column A is whether they want to go on vacation or not. If they decide together that they can't talk at all about vacation until they discuss money, then money moves to column A, and they meet about that. If they decide instead that for this meeting they still want to think only about different vacation possibilities, then maybe they will handle the financial concerns in their next meeting. (Don't be discouraged if, early in this process, you need a meeting or two just to decide on the topics for your meetings!)

Note taking forces your brain to focus and organize while you are documenting what was said.[3] Use the notes to keep checking that you're on track. You can also use the notepad as another method for self-soothing. Writing, or even just doodling, can calm you a bit while you try to stay focused. Any knitter or wood-carver knows the soothing affect of keeping one's hands busy.

3. **Set time limits.** I encourage couples to limit their most important or difficult conversations to half-hour increments. Most people truly have difficulty concentrating and focusing at their best for longer than that. This limit also offers a useful checkpoint to see

whether you are actually accomplishing anything or whether you're just stuck. When you are in important discussions, the body and mind seek relief, and a time constraint can be an impersonal and structured limit on your ability to hurt each other. A buzzer going off or the clock striking the half-hour point imposes a limit on the amount of damage you can do.

Many couples proudly report to me that they've been able to have a very productive discussion that lasted for three or more hours. I'm always congratulatory, because the fact that they were willing to hang in there and talk is in itself a success. (They may not remember all they talked about, and they may disagree on the outcome later, but nevertheless they've had a success.) You may find, however, that after about twenty or thirty minutes, you begin to repeat yourself, raise your voice, or become confused. You now know that these are symptoms of the Reptilian Brain taking over.

The time limit allows both of you to know that you will need to work quickly and accurately in order to get in your most important points. This in turn discourages you from introducing other topics that will confuse and delay the discussion. Finally, for the partner who dreads and avoids long, drawn-out discussions, it offers a predictable ending, which means that some portion of the evening will be free for other activities.

If you agree to place a time limit on your partnership meetings, a further point bears mention: consider two time limits! Now you may be saying, "Oh no, he's making it more complicated," but actually it's easy, and it helps you stick to the half-hour limit. All I'm suggesting is that if you're planning on a half-hour discussion, leave the last five minutes for making agreements and contracts for further action or discussion. These last few minutes of the meeting can be the part of the meeting where you (1) review any agreements so far and (2) decide what you need to do next. You may finish a topic in half an hour, but that's not always possible (or necessary). If the subject does require more time, you need to know that you're not being cut off and that further discussion will take place. With this commitment, you should be able to move on to other chores or pleasures for that day and get some sleep that night.

4. **Schedule breaks.** Taking breaks is important. If you find reptilian responses kicking in, you must be able to take time out. The length of the break and how it's spent may be quite different for different couples. Is this a twenty-minute break to have a glass of water, calm down, and think a bit? Do you need a few days to gather additional information or think about the problem? The main point is that the break should serve as a continuation of the problem-solving approach and not just as a form of flight. During the break in a difficult discussion, a good question to ask yourself is, "What do I need in order to feel good about this issue?"

5. **Agree on how to end the discussion.** Many people continue discussing and fighting because they have no way to judge when they've come to a stopping point. Some people simply stop talking, walk away, or slam a door—but what does this tell the partner? Are you leaving her? Are you going to call an attorney or an old lover? Are you going to hold this against him forever and never speak to him again? Human beings, by and large, cannot tolerate these kinds of uncertainties. Such unanswered questions will increase the anxiety of the one who is left behind. Often the one who leaves knows he hasn't done well and will be more likely to respond aggressively upon his return or when this subject resurfaces. The foundation for the next reptilian battle has already been laid. If partners can agree on how to let go of an argument, understanding that they still care and that they just need a break, they'll be able to relax. If your partner said, "Look I know this is important to you and it is to me, too, but I am out of steam right now. Can we do this again tomorrow at the same time," would you find that comforting? Such information should allow you to leave the argument without injuring each other and return to it in a more productive fashion. Perhaps the best place to first practice ending discussions well will be in these scheduled semiformal meetings. Eventually you will want to expand this behavior of ending discussions well to all of your challenging interactions.

Evolutionary Tip
Learn to Use Nonverbal Signals

Often when you try to stop an argument verbally, your language actually exacerbates the argument. Some couples benefit from nonverbal signals, such as the common time-out signal in sports. You and your partner should agree in advance on the signal and its exact meaning. If you perceive your partner as giving the time-out signal and meaning, "This discussion is over and I win," you won't be able to respect the signal. If you agree that the time-out signal means, for example, "I'm exhausted. I need ten minutes to collect my thoughts and be a friendlier human being," then you are still in communication.

You have a thousand such signals between you already, many of which you may not consciously notice. You know that when he stands a certain way it means he's angry. When she uses that nickname it means she's feeling good about you. So now, purposefully give some of your signals meaning that only the two of you understand.

PARTNERSHIP MEETINGS
DON'T GET PERSONAL

As you meet, you should be thinking about whether you're handling business or personal issues. Unfortunately, when most people fight, they start out talking business, but soon switch to personal attacks. "We need to figure out which one of these bills we should pay first" is business. "We have too many bills because you spend money like a drunken sailor" is personal. Even something as intimate as sexuality can be viewed in this manner. Are you talking about wanting to have more interesting sexual encounters, or are you talking about some kinds of problems that you perceive in each other? Such a discussion might be rather businesslike in terms of trying to decide on better times to attempt sexual intimacy and whether to incorporate books or toys. It might, however, focus on something more personal to one or both of you that is seen as preventing intimacy. Are one of you depressed or stressed out? Do one of you have an irritating habit that is a sexual turnoff?

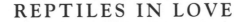

REPTILES IN LOVE
What You Do to Me

Nat and Aretha had been fighting more than usual. Nat described his anger at having Aretha treat him like "some kind of criminal" when all he wanted was to talk to her or touch her. This was worse when he tried to approach her affectionately. For example, she was looking in the closet when he walked into the bedroom and said, "You look hot tonight." She jerked as though she'd been struck and said, "If you keep doing that, I'm going to hang a bell on you. Could you maybe give me a little warning before rushing at me?" Nat felt that every part of this was unfair, and he resented that his trying to give Aretha a compliment had been totally lost on her. They then got into a heated battle about whether Nat wasn't careful enough and whether Aretha was too sensitive and high-strung.

This discussion, of course, was hopeless. Nat had no intention of harming Aretha, but when he defended himself, he seemed to be saying that something was wrong with her. Aretha, who had always been startled easily, was embarrassed by her anxious reactions. The combination of fear and humiliation that occurred each time this happened predicated an angry response. Knowing that Nat thought she was a "Nervous Nellie," as her father used to call her, made her

(continued on next page)

(continued)

REPTILES IN LOVE
What You Do to Me

feel weak and ineffective. When she accused Nat of sneaking up on her, she sounded as though she thought he were a bad guy, "like some kind of stalker." They both felt accused and demeaned, and subsequently felt the need to attack and defend.

Nat and Aretha's confrontation seems like an intensely personal confrontation. Yet we were quickly able to turn this into an agenda item for Nat and Aretha's partnership meeting. With structure and specific questions, Aretha and Nat began to talk about their accusations and injuries. They reassured each other that they cared deeply, and began to strategize about Aretha's startle response (some education about startle responses and anxiety was very helpful in terms of making this a more businesslike discussion).[4]

Nat and Aretha quickly came up with a plan that included several key points. One specific issue was that if Nat did accidentally startle Aretha, he would simply back up and give her a moment to collect herself. He learned that the startle reaction was physical in nature and not something directed at him. Aretha realized that Nat was not intentionally surprising her; therefore, there was no need to make such accusations. They both knew that slowing down the rush of reactions with each other would take some practice, but the fact that they were collaborating instead of accusing made this now seem possible.

Don't Shut Down Just Because You Disagree

We have responses, verbal or behavioral, that serve to stop our partners from communicating with us. Those responses often suggest that we feel superior in terms of intelligence, morality, upbringing, or maturity. If your partner talks to you in a way that sounds like a parent or teacher—particularly if he or she sounds too much like one of your parents or a least favorite teacher—you're likely to feel silenced and shut down. You will not want to continue the communication because you feel personally attacked or hopeless to really be able to succeed in communicating effectively. You have seen from earlier discussions of the Reptilian Response that neither is likely to learn anything new at this point in the discussion.

Shut-down language can also include the *way* you say things, in terms of tone or body language. For example, if you display the characteristic smirk or eye roll, which universally conveys contempt for what your partner is saying, then you'll likely make any further attempts at communication impossible. What kind of language or behavior works as a shut-down for you and your partner? Review the list that follows; which behaviors do you use to shut down your partner? How do you see your partner shutting you down?

Dismissal	Leaving the room
	Placing a newspaper, book, or other object in front of you
	Making displays of contempt: smirk, eye roll, dismissive hand gesture, and so on
	Laughing derisively
Aggression	Sarcasm
	Raised voice
	Physical intimidation (invading personal space, threats)
	Insults
	Talking as though to a child
Diagnosis	"You're this way because you [are male, female, depressed, alcoholic, stressed out,

or crazy or have Attention Deficit Disorder, PMS . . .].”

“You’re this way because of your family.”

“You’re just like your [mother, father, and so on].

One-upping	“I’m smarter than you.”
	“Here are my credentials.”
	“I’ve read more than you.”
	“I watch *Oprah*.”
	“Experts agree with me.”

The goal in identifying shut-down language and behaviors is to raise them to a conscious level for both partners. These behaviors, though maddening, are often largely unintentional. They’re automatic habits of speech or behavior your partner may not recognize as self-defeating. Often when partners confront each other on shut-down behaviors, their aggressive approach pushes the partner into a defensive posture. Instead, talk about these habits in a calm, rational manner during a partnership meeting, explaining how they affect you. If you do, perhaps your partner, who when fearful begins to speak to you as though you were a five-year-old, will approach you with more awareness. You might then also recognize that this is a nervous reaction and not an attack on your intelligence. Once you’ve both gained this understanding, in the future you can remind him in a kind way, “You’re using that voice again” (rather than screaming, *Don’t talk to me that way!*”), and move on with a more efficient discussion.

Learn How to Negotiate

A noted negotiator was doing some deep-sea fishing when he caught a large, rather amazing-looking fish. He’d never seen anything like this colorful giant and was even more amazed when, writhing in agony, it spoke to him.

"Release me back into the water, and I'll grant you three wishes," the fish gasped.

"What kind of sucker do you take me for? Make it five wishes, and I'll do as you say," replied the shrewd negotiator.

"No, only three wishes. I'm sorry, but that's the limit."

The negotiator was determined not to be outdone by a fish, so he countered, "Let's make it four wishes."

The fish cried out, "No, I told you I can do only three."

This was indeed a bind. The negotiator was beaten and finally said, "Okay, I'll take the three wishes. But let's keep this between us. The guys at the office would laugh their heads off if they heard I was outmaneuvered by a fish."

But by that time, of course, the fish was dead.

What are you supposed to do when the two of you get stuck and can neither agree nor comfort each other? Here's a little tip from the field of business and political negotiations: When you hit such a spot in negotiations, you must back up to something on which the two of you can agree. I tell couples that everything is negotiable. This is of course a bit of an exaggeration, but I do want them to know that there are a lot of things that *are* negotiable, once both partners are in a nonreptilian state that allows them to look for creative ways to solve their problems. I'm reminded of a joke about Siamese twins who moved to England so the other one could drive for a while—a creative response to a seemingly impossible request.

In a pitched battle, partners may be able to agree only that her feelings were hurt and that he's sorry that it happened. But hey— that's not bad; they agreed on two things! This initial understanding already puts them far beyond arguing about his being a jerk and her being too sensitive. They might then be able to move forward without such accusations toward some means of preventing such behaviors in the future.

Let's try an almost impossibly hot topic. Two people are fighting over custody issues in their divorce. They certainly don't agree on which one of them is the better parent, which has the best home environment, who will spend the most quality time with the children, or who has the better spiritual values. In backing up through all these subjects, they may have to return repeatedly to the one basic truth on which they can agree: they don't want the children to be unduly harmed by their divorce. They might further agree that a long, vicious battle will most likely harm their children. They might then agree that their name-calling and insults make it impossible for them to treat their children well. They may reluctantly recognize that bad-mouthing the other parent is having a terrible effect on the children. You will find further discussion of divorce in Chapter Ten and there is a divorce section in the Resources.

At this point, one of them—it doesn't matter who, because they take turns going on the attack anyway—suggests that it is the other who starts with the insults and therefore doesn't care enough about the children and will probably end up selling them into slavery. Sure it's nasty, but it's also pretty normal. At such times, they will again need to back up to where they can both recognize that this will not help and to examine whether there is another direction they can go. Perhaps their resentment is so strong that they simply will never be able to agree that the other is a good and caring parent. Still, they may be able to recognize that they don't want to hurt the children or use all their children's college funds for lawyers and court proceedings.

Now let's look at a more moderate negotiation, in this case a fantasy wish. Jacquelyn asks Joe, "Can't we please dress nicely for dinner sometimes?" Joe, sensing a trap, replies, "Look, I know I'm not as fine as some of your friends, but I'm comfortable, and I'm not going to wear some damned monkey suit just to get a meal around here." Jacquelyn then opts to defend her friends. "You're always putting down anyone I like. You act as if we're all snobs. It wouldn't kill you to put on some clean sweatpants now and then, Joe."

This couple is, of course, on the wrong subject—but if they back up a bit, they might be able to ask a simple question. For example, what is it that Jacquelyn actually wants? Jacquelyn has always loved movies where people are dressed up in finery. She has a fantasy of a date in which Joe would wear a jacket and tie, and they would have candles and music and really make a big deal out of dinner. She wouldn't want to do this too often, because frankly it sounds like a lot of work. Every time she begins to tell Joe about this idea, he thinks she's comparing him to some of her "fancy friends." He sometimes gets the idea that she wishes she would have married someone like them. It's a scary thought, and it makes him angry.

The negotiation in this case is simply a matter of getting to the details of what Jacquelyn wants. Joe says, "If you think I'm dressing up every other night after a long day at work, you've got another think coming."

That's when Jacquelyn, realizing that Joe thinks she's asking for a lot more than she really wants, slows things down and says, "Wait a minute. I don't want you to dress up often. I'd just like to spend a little special time with you. Are you interested in spending time with me?" This is the important negotiation question: "Do we agree that we would like to be together?" If Joe agrees, then they move ahead. If he doesn't, then they first have to explore why not.

So now let's say that they agree they should spend more time together. Jacquelyn forges ahead: "Maybe once a month or so. I'd like you to dress up and make a real date out of dinner together. I want you to sit with me at dinner and tell me I look nice, and I'll tell you that you look nice."

Joe now has an actual proposal on the table. He might ask a question: "If we plan this, and one of us can't do it, how big a deal is that going to be?"

She spots an attempted escape. "What are you saying? You'll promise now, and then back out at the last minute?"

Okay, he should have seen that coming, so he continues, "No. I will do dinner, but only once a month to begin with. I'll commit to being there, and it will take an enormous conflict or illness to make me ask for a rain check. If something does happen, I *will* give you a rain check. I will owe you the evening, so it won't help me to try to duck out."

She likes most of this, but replies, "You make this sound like a horrible chore."

"Well, I'm not thrilled with dressing up, but I do want to spend more time with you," says Joe. "Let's just see how it works a couple times."

The process of negotiation lessens the need for an attack-defend mentality. The technique of backing to a point of agreement, from where the couple becomes stuck, allows them to then work forward again cooperatively. They can then again work toward resolving that specific point of stuckness before moving on. You'll see negotiations discussed in many contexts in this book because almost everything is negotiable once you develop a sense of trust and safety.

FACING MAJOR CHANGES

Paul came home from his physical looking completely devastated.

Nancy asked, "My God, what's wrong with you?"

Paul replied, "The doc says I've got to take one of these pills every day for the rest of my life."

"Well, come on," Nancy exclaimed. "That's not so bad. A lot of people need to take medication."

"I know that," he snapped, "but he gave me only four pills."

We can't always control what happens in our lives. Sometimes the things we have to negotiate are related to major life changes—a death in the family, an unexpected pregnancy, a sudden change in financial situation, a different job, a move to a new house or a new state. How do you deal with the issues that surround these kinds of events? Here are some tips for organizing your thoughts and meetings:

1. **Communicate, communicate, communicate.** Let each other know what's going on and how you intend to help each other. Talk about the problem as if it were outside your relationship by considering the forces operating against the two of you instead of focus-

ing on which one of you is to blame for the immediate feelings. Use language that defines the two of you as a team up against a common enemy. For example, in dealing with something as potentially touchy as an in-law problem, you can choose to describe how awful your partner's family member is, or you can ask your partner how to handle the awkward things that occur around that person. Which do you think your partner will be more likely to hear and respect?

Often a very simple acknowledgment of the problem—"I need some time to think about it"—is all you need to say at the moment. Partners often hesitate to communicate with each other until they are sure of themselves, especially when facing big issues. They want to have all their ducks in a row and not say anything they can't prove. This is particularly true in highly competitive relationships. But if you don't communicate in some way that you have heard your partner and considered her concerns, she'll have no sense of ongoing cooperation. You don't need to give the perfect answer or even any answer if you at least let her know that you're going to return with something. This reminds her that she's important to you and is not being ignored.

Saying "Leave me alone" or "I'm not going to talk to you about that" or simply walking away provides no agreement or comfort and no relief of tension. When you're finally ready to return to the issue, you'll find your partner more anxious or upset than she was before.

2. **Forecast and anticipate change.** Try to describe each way in which the change will affect your relationship and what you will have to do to protect it. Just saying, "Hey, it will be okay" will probably not help. Vague reassurance can be comforting, but it isn't as helpful as a serious assessment of how your relationship will be affected by the change. Even if there are several potential negatives, you can deal with them more effectively as a team if you openly acknowledge them.

So, for instance, when a couple is preparing for their first child, they're often reluctant to talk about how they're going to miss being a twosome. They might feel a little selfish to say that they'll miss being able to have sex or go out any time they want. They may be reluctant to discuss their fears of whether they will be able to be good parents. In another example, a move to a new city will result in different friends, travel schedules, housing, time demands—and who knows what else. If fears of the unknown remain unspoken, they develop potentially disastrous power. I believe couples always do better when they actually try to review the downsides and threats to their relationship posed by any major change. It's far better to ask yourselves, "What's the worst thing that could happen?" (and realize you can survive that) than to simply say, "Everything will turn out fine."

3. **Communicate empathy.** Let your partner know that you care about what he's going through. Often we try too hard to be reassuring, but come across as if we're not seeing the problem. "Hey, your new job means I won't be seeing you except on weekends, but I don't mind" is not a message a partner wants to hear. False reassurances and half-truths rarely help. They're like having a doctor tell you, "This isn't going to hurt a bit." You know it's just talk. You need to tell your partner that you care that he's hurt or scared and that he's not wrong for feeling that way.

4. **Promise only what you can deliver.** Much like false reassurances, false promises are not helpful. "I will fix everything" is a promise we rarely can keep. Most often we're not even sure of what needs fixing, because we haven't asked.

5. **Don't take responsibility for your partner's reactions to the problem.** A most common trap for loving partners is to feel responsible for their partner's feelings (see Chapter Three). They believe that if their partner is unhappy, it's a reflection of their failings as a partner.

6. **Be willing to review your agreements or understandings.** You need to be willing to ask whether you still have similar goals and whether you accurately perceive your partner's needs. Have any needs or goals changed for either of you? Everything is an experiment and so your plans will need to be reviewed after a few weeks

or months to see if they still work. For example, you might ask your partner to spend fifteen minutes talking to you as soon as she comes home from work, every single evening. Eventually you discover that this feels too stilted or formal and also creates frustration because things get in the way. You notice that you actually feel better as long as there is some form of greeting when you first see each other and this small agreement seems to allow you to engage more easily with each other throughout the rest of the evening.

Throughout this chapter, you've been learning the art and skill of communication: how to get all the reptilian nonsense out of the way so that you can talk about the real issues that are affecting your relationship. Up to this point, however, we've taken only on-the-surface looks at what those deeper issues might be. In the next chapter, we'll talk about how to describe, define, and deal with specific problems in your relationship.

5

Step Three
Clarify Your Needs and Fears Together

*Ralph is walking home after several hours in the local
tavern and stumbles into a tree. He backs up and
lurches forward, only to run right back into the same
tree. He does this a couple more times. "Oh, this is
just great," he says. "I was supposed to be home
hours ago, and here I am lost in a forest."*

You now understand how the Reptilian Brain works and why you
sometimes hurt or ignore those you care most about. You have
evaluated yourself and will continue to do so, and are watching your
level of stress and emotional arousal throughout the day. You may
even have started doing some relaxation exercises or using other
stress management techniques. You now also understand that you
and your partner have developed inaccurate and unhelpful stories
about each other and your relationship. You have begun having
organized meetings with your partner. You're getting much closer to
reducing the power the Reptilian Brain holds in your intimate relationship. But you're not there yet.

In this chapter, you will practice focusing your efforts on the specific issues facing your relationship. You'll learn how to clarify and
define just what it is you're afraid of and what it is you need from
yourself and from your partner to make this relationship work. You'll
quiet your impulse to perceive every remark or behavior as an

attack, and learn to identify those areas that most need attention from each of you for the relationship. Organizing your thoughts in this manner engages your higher brain capacities, which allows you to be curious and creative about marital issues instead of being fearful and guarded.[1]

DEFINING YOUR PROBLEMS

How do you define the specific problems in your relationship? The common areas of disagreement surround money, sex, and children, closely followed by concerns about the use of time, sharing of jobs, and relationships (of all kinds) with other people. These topics, however, often miss the more central issue of whether the partners feel loved, respected, and safe with each other.

Finding Out What You and Your Partner Really Need

In all matters of opinion, our adversaries are insane.
Mark Twain

Couples have many ways of arguing about everything under the sun except what is most bothering them. They often focus on surface issues in order to avoid stepping on land mines. The following are two of the most common ways in which they avoid getting to the real issues:

- *It's all your [my] fault.* Do you sometimes think that your partner was put on this earth to make you miserable? Do you get the feeling that he or she wakes up every morning with but one thought: "How can I drive my partner crazy today?" Or do you suppose that *you* are the entire problem in the relationship and that it's a wonder your partner stays with you at all? Have you said to yourself, "If I wasn't so bad [depressed, anxious, tired, homely, stupid, lazy], my partner would be hap-

pier and everything would be okay"? Defining your
problems by focusing solely on one half of your partnership will generally not help you change negative feelings, communications, or behaviors. In fact, such
one-sided definitions can only make things worse.

- *Missing the forest for the trees.* It's easy to become overwhelmed when you start to think about relationship
  problems. Where do you begin? Like the intoxicated
  Ralph at the beginning of the chapter, many despairing
  couples may feel as though they're lost in a forest of
  troubles when in fact they just keep running into the
  same old tree. It's frightening to think you'll have to
  have meetings about every aspect of your lives in order
  to tolerate each other.

Fear not! It really is possible to let go of both these fears and sort
things out. To start, choose one issue that is important to both of
you and that both of you can resolve (for example, to stop calling
each other "stupid" when you disagree). For a brief time, try to block
out every other issue and focus on just that one target. This may
also be an exchange of requests, such as, "I will stop raising my
voice, and I'd like you not to mention my family." If you can bring
about even a tiny change in one area, you've been successful. Success breeds success; as your trust in each other grows, other problems will also seem solvable. You may take only a small step, but it's
a way to start.

Once you've stopped being overwhelmed by seemingly insur-
mountable problems and stopped blaming yourself or your partner
for everything that goes wrong, you can start to do the work necessary to find out what you and your partner really need to discuss.
Often we find that our arguments focus on issues that are neither
critical nor helpful to us. We're not even sure why they seemed like
such a big deal at the time.

The *real* issues are those that matter: What do you really, really, really need from your partner? What do you need him or her to say to you? What will make you feel safe and loved? What will make you excited to see your partner? What would make sex seem like a good idea? If your arguments don't come close to answering any of these questions, then they're the wrong discussions.

To define your problems, you've got to become more scientific in approaching your relationship. You need to learn to discount superficial accusations or confrontations that have no basis in reality, and instead listen for what's beneath the surface, for deeper information that your partner is expressing about what he or she really wants. For instance, suppose your partner were to say to you, "Let's go out, just the two of us. You never want to go out or do anything anymore. You only want to be with the children. You're so boring. I feel like I'm in prison here." You could decide to respond to this "attack" with the usual defenses: "Can't you see that I'm tired? I do all the housework, and I work at my job too. I'm the only one who takes care of the kids, since you never pay them any attention." Your partner has blamed the problem on you, and you've accepted his framing of the situation. Therefore, it's only natural for you to defend yourself and counterattack.[2]

But if you succumb to such a defensive reaction to what your partner is saying, then you've lost sight of the underlying positive part of his request—that he would like to spend more time alone with you. If you can instead agree that you've had less time together and less of a social life since the children were born and that you'd both really like to have more quality time together, then you have a goal on which to collaborate and a place at which to begin the problem-solving process.

When couples come to me for therapy, I tell them that I'm not going to focus on either one of them much individually. Instead, I'm going to look at their relationship. When I tell them that we're going to define problems as stemming from the contract they've made with each other and not necessarily as related to either one of them personally, they're usually relieved. Problems are best addressed when defined "outside" the couple; the more personalized the definition, the less likely the partner is to hear the complaint and make changes.

Saying, "You're lazy and never help around the house," won't lead to change. The only message that comes through is, "You're not good enough. I don't love you," even though that's not what was said. It might be better to say something about your own feelings: "We never seem to be able to keep up with everything around here. Can we talk about how to get more out of our lives?" This may still raise some suspicions, but at least it invites discussion. It suggests that you haven't already defined your partner as the problem.

If you say, "Our sex life has sure slowed down. You never seem interested," you're obviously suggesting that there's something wrong with your partner. You know by now that this will automatically instill in your partner a physical need to defend himself or to pull away. He's not turning a deaf ear; he simply can't hear you and won't be able to respond to what you really want. Try saying instead, "It seems like we're not as close as we used to be. We hardly ever touch each other, and we don't have sex as much as we used to. I'd like to talk about how we spend time together and how we can get close again." This opens the door to talking about anything that might be blocking affection and intimacy.

Finding Out What You and Your Partner Really Fear

It is difficult—but crucial—to recognize that most of your disagreements are about the wrong thing. They're symbolic of other problems that are less accessible or are difficult to identify. This chapter is dedicated to encouraging the two of you to work very hard on discussing the true nature of your disagreements, the real needs and fears, including all the details and underlying issues.

For example, let's suppose you argue with your partner about the party you went to on Saturday night, where he spent forty-five minutes talking to your neighbor's attractive cousin, in a pretty cozy,

flirtatious manner. Is this argument about your mistrust of your partner and the cousin—or is it about your fear of not feeling safe and
loved? Those are different subjects. Is the question whether your
husband is a philanderer who would rather be with other women?
Is it really that when he flirts, you fear that he doesn't love or appreciate you anymore, or doesn't think that you're still attractive? Or
is it that you've been feeling disconnected from him and lonely?

The first question is investigative and about control. The second refers to your own anxiety about your attractiveness and his
commitment. The third is seeking connection and is probably going to be the most helpful in rebuilding your relationship, even
though you may not be able to discard the first two completely. The
"symbol" in this case is your partner's flirting at the party. The real
issue is that you fear you're drifting apart. (This is not to ignore the
fact that the act of flirting is a signal of availability to infidelity,
which is dangerous to the relationship. Even when the flirtatious
partner doesn't think he's serious about offering such an invitation,
he's sending a mixed message to you as well as to the target of his
flirting.[3])

Your Reptilian Brain wants to accuse and attack your partner
rather than face the possibility that the distance you feel is really
there. That would hurt, and your Reptilian Brain wants to shield
you from pain. The irony is, however, that only when you and your
partner acknowledge the distance can you begin to close it. Being
able to directly address a disconnection allows healing to begin.

Let's take another tough example of a symbolic theme: money.[4]
Along with children and sex, money ranks as one of the most common themes of relationship battle. The conflict over money can be
further broken down into the following complaints:

- One partner spends more than is acceptable.

- One has more control over the checkbook or credit
  cards than the other.

- One complains about costs every time they go out, and the other feels devalued.

- One brought more money or goods into the relationship than the other.

- One brought more problems, debts, children, or expenses into the relationship.

Whatever the complaint, if the concern keeps coming up in the relationship and the couple cannot effectively address it, then they're probably on the wrong subject. Money *always* represents other issues and fears in a relationship.[5] In other words, if money were a simple business issue of how much a couple can afford to spend, the partners would just do the math and come to an agreement. But money represents power, freedom, control, and self-determination. How partners discuss and manage money will predict whether they feel loved, respected, and trusted. When a person describes his partner as being frivolous or irresponsible with money, he doesn't see her as his equal, or he fears that she may somehow undermine his authority and control. This is not to ignore real financial concerns but to underline the issues that prevent them from actively talking about these concerns.

When couples return repeatedly to the theme of who earns the most, who spends the most, and who is the most fiscally capable, they're marking their territory. Does this mean that a person must simply ignore a partner who is wildly spending and driving them into financial ruin, or, conversely, appreciate the partner who feverishly counts out their expenses to the penny? No, not at all! But you must understand that attacking each other's personal beliefs or anxieties in this realm will also not work. Finances are a powerful force and must be approached with considerable respect and caution.

It doesn't help to make such statements to your partner as "You're so cheap, we'd live in a tent if you had your way" or "You're spending us into the poorhouse." When one person spends too much or too little, it may be because he was very poor as a child, was afraid of being poor when growing up, or is mimicking values he got from his parents—or it may be related to realistic fears about a current financial situation. If you're constantly sending the message that he's sick or bad for worrying, he will worry more.

While you're busy criticizing his views on money, he may fear that you're out of control and are placing the family at risk, when all you're really trying to do is protect the family in your own way. Once you both see that your needs are based on fears, values, and early learning, you may be able to help each other calm down and become a bit more playful. Here is one approach you can take:

1. Decide together what your actual financial concerns and goals are. This may be a discussion you've never had. Are you saving for your children's college education? How much money do each of you feel you need to have in the bank for emergencies? How do each of you feel about credit card debt?[6]

2. This discussion, without blame or accusations, should lead into negotiations of your actual differences. For example, your partner may find any credit card debt to be unacceptable, whereas you believe that all couples have debt. You might be able to agree on an upper limit of debt and that you won't keep any credit card that charges a high interest rate.

3. As we discussed in the section on negotiations in Chapter Four, whenever you reach a point of disagreement or become reptilian, take a break or back up to whatever points of agreement you have reached and see what facts pull you apart.

A necessary step in all these interactions is for you to remind yourselves that this should be a "business" discussion and not about personal shortcomings. You will be best able to reach a conclusion that works for both of you if you leave personal interpretations and accusations out of the discussion completely.

FIVE WAYS TO DISCOVER WHAT YOU'RE REALLY FIGHTING ABOUT

Think about something that you and your partner fight about all the time. Is it a subject that raises your defensive instincts and makes you feel hopeless or unheard? If so, there's almost certainly a pattern to it. If you look at your cycle of repeated disagreements or challenges, you'll notice that there isn't simply a single straightforward argument occurring—the two of you are actually introducing a number of points and needs. The goal is to separate the issues, listen, and deal with them one at a time without either partner having to score his or her own points. There are several ways to accomplish this goal, and we'll look at each of them:

1. Practice nondefensive listening.
2. Watch your language.
3. Establish importance by playing the numbers game.
4. Keep it brief.
5. Don't fill in the blanks, and don't make your partner fill them in either.

Practice Nondefensive Listening

Nondefensive, or active, listening requires a great deal of courage, and it becomes easier as trust between you grows. It means that you don't immediately take responsibility for your partner and that you refuse to defend yourself. Remember, if one of you feels the need to defend yourself, the discussion is already over, because your Reptilian Brain has overrun your ability to listen.

Nondefensive listening is possible only when you can assume that your partner is not going to harm you. This means that you must ignore (for the time being) any insulting or scary comments from your partner. You'll still need to insist that such negative behavior must stop, but for now you'll be listening for what it is that your partner truly needs or fears.

Just because you're feeling attacked at any given moment doesn't mean that your partner is in fact attacking. She may actually want you to accept her opinion—without your feeling attacked—even if it's critical of you (because that means you trust and respect her). You might first check with each other as to whether what you're arguing about is the real issue; otherwise your discussion will be a waste of time.

Evolutionary Tip
The Active-Listening Exercise

There is an exercise you can do that takes about a half hour to complete. Begin by having your partner explain a concern to you for ten minutes. (You may wish to use the "unspeakable subjects" format offered at the end of this chapter.) Don't interrupt and don't defend yourself.[7] What does your partner really want from you? Does she want you to just listen, or is she expecting some action? Most often it will be best if you can simply ask this directly but avoid any hint of sarcasm. Your partner is more likely to feel listened to if you can honestly ask, "What do you most need from me during this discussion?" Screen out anything that sounds like a personal attack; you can deal with that another time. Right now, just listen for what she really needs and take some time to sit with it. Don't answer right away (this will be hard).

When she's finished, restate to her what you understand her concerns to be, without commentary and without sarcasm.

Now it's your turn. For ten minutes, explain a concern to your partner. Try to use "I" statements, such as "I need more time with you," rather than "You never do anything with me." Eliminate personal criticisms and focus only on what you need.

When you're finished, have her restate what she understands your concerns to be.

When you're both finished, take a break and sit with this information for a time before responding. You both may need a few minutes or a day to digest what has been said and to think about whether you can meet any of the needs your partner has expressed.

Watch Your Language

Most couples think they understand each other linguistically. I find that this is rarely the case. People hear things quite differently. They make huge assumptions and feel betrayed when they find out that what they thought they heard is not what the other person thought he or she said. A little clarity could cut down on unpleasant surprises and provide considerable relief.

In therapy I repeatedly ask couples to be clear and specific in the meanings of their words, requests, complaints, and goals. Suppose your partner says, "We should go out more often." What exactly does "more often" mean? How often do you think you should do something with your partner alone? How often with the kids, friends, or other family members? What does "doing something" mean? Is cleaning the kitchen together "doing something"? Being as specific as possible is also important because partners generally define each other with terms implying immovability. "She *always* does this to me." "He *never* does anything I like."

Seeking clarity also means asking your partner about the true nature of his or her upsetting statement or question. This is simple in concept, yet it is difficult to do. "That comment really stung. Was it meant to hurt?" would be a wonderful question. Notice how this feels compared to "Why do you *always* have to talk to me that way?"

That kind of question usually leads to what I call a red herring argument. In a mystery story, a clue or concept that sounds like a plausible course of investigation but that actually leads the detective down the wrong path is called a red herring. In an argument, the red herring is the subject that leads both partners down the wrong path. In this example, it may sound to both partners as if they need to solve whether the one always talks "that way," when in fact the more important issue is that at this specific moment, one partner felt hurt by something the other said.

Clarifying the meaning of words is extremely important and takes a lot of practice. If the focus stays on whether the one partner "always talks that way," this becomes a challenge as to whether one or both of them are deficient human beings. In other words, is the one partner who "talks that way" just a mean, nasty, sadistic person? Is the other partner "too sensitive"? Rather than solving a problem, this exchange can have only one possible conclusion: that one of them must be wrong and therefore not a good, smart, or competent person. I have never seen a relationship improve because one of the partners was proved wrong or bad. It is an impossible and unrewarding task, and therefore such discussions are potentially endless.

Establish Importance by Playing the Numbers Game

Relationship problems often arise because couples misjudge how important a particular issue is to one of the partners. Your partner wants to go out for dinner and thinks this is a simple request that should be easy for you to honor. He's hurt and angry when you say that you're tired and would rather that he pick up some takeout on the way home. Then he says that he's not running a delivery service and would really rather go out, and you each perceive the other as being uncooperative and childish.

One way to clarify importance is to use a simple rating device, such as a 1–10 rating scale. An intensity level of 1 would suggest, "This issue has virtually no importance to me whatsoever, and I'm perfectly happy to go along with you on this." An intensity level of 10 suggests, "This is so important to me that I may stop breathing, and humanity as we know it will be negatively affected if I don't get my way." The numbers in the center of this continuum might say to the partner that the other would prefer a specific solution or direction, but are open to negotiation.

Obviously a lot of trust goes into using this scale effectively. Partners need to know that they are both trying to be as accurate and as honest as they can be in identifying their issues. Both need to remember that there's nothing scientific about such a scale. It's merely a means of conveying a piece of information.

So let's replay the conversation you and your partner might have about going out to eat. You might say that you're really tired, but that staying home is only a 5 on the 1–10 scale. He might counter that going out to eat is very important to him at this particular moment, maybe as high as an 8. You decide that because he's been pretty good at using this scale, something must be up, and you agree to go out. He might then reveal at dinner that he's just gotten a big promotion and is planning to buy some cattle for your backyard. You're glad you didn't miss this event, and he's glad he didn't have to make such a heady announcement over a bag of tacos.

The scale allows you to give initial information about how you're reading a situation without immediately needing to defend yourself, whine about how you don't ask for much, or complain about your partner. Notice that this scale is a mechanical, artificial, and dispassionate means of helping you pick your battles. There are no explanations necessary. It's simply a way to disengage your reptilian response (reptiles can't count) and gauge your partner's emotional investment in the issue currently on the table.

Keep It Brief

As important as being clear and specific is to good nonreptilian communication, limiting your language to the most critical information can help get you through complicated or frightening discussions.

REPTILES IN LOVE
Chewing the Fat and Eating Crow

Harry and Sally were among several friends at a dinner party at Dave and Becky's home. Harry happened to mention during dinner that Sally's "few extra pounds" since the birth of their son have just made her cuddlier. Everyone laughed. On the way home, Harry declares what a great time he had. No response.

Sally was boiling like Louisiana jambalaya. Can we really blame her? Her attack went something like this:

"What the hell is wrong with you? Why would you make such a stupid remark? If you want to complain about me being fat, maybe you could do that here instead of announcing it to the whole neighborhood. What are you trying to do? You seemed to spend a lot of time talking to Becky. What's going on with that? Do you even care about me at all anymore? You don't seem to think about my feelings. Is it possible that you were dropped on your head as a child, and it's been kept a secret this long? If you think I'm too fat for you, why don't you just say so and go find yourself a thinner, younger model?"

This is actually a brief and censored version of her entire sermon. What would you view as her actual message or feeling? It's hidden in there somewhere. I would guess that the entire program could have been boiled down to "Do you even care about me anymore?" The problem is that after the first few words, Harry stopped listening and went into defensive mode. All he could think was, "Boy, all she ever does these days is get angry at the smallest little thing!"

Brief, clear messages are more likely to be listened to and understood than long, convoluted descriptions. In his book *How to Get Your Point Across in 30 Seconds or Less*, Milo Franks notes that advertisers, politicians, and businesspeople have known for years that people have approximately thirty-second attention spans and can only manage a few concepts at a time.[8] This time and subject limit decreases under stress.

This means that during a stressful event, a message of importance to an intimate partner needs to be produced in considerably less than thirty seconds! Of course, this is asking an awful lot of a person who is riled up, hurt, or scared. But think about what happens when the message is too long or complicated.

When you send several messages at once, your partner is likely to miss the most important point. She may select the most dramatic, frightening, or urgent point—or, conversely, she may pick out the bit of information that's easiest to manage. Harry hears the question about his interest in Becky. He's comfortable in denying that, because it isn't true. He thinks for a moment, "My gosh, Becky's even bigger than Sally." He is very fortunate to not have mentioned this insight. He doesn't notice when Sally says, "Do you even care about me at all anymore?" because that's a more difficult subject right now. It's a question that poses danger, so he literally doesn't hear it.

We all have selective hearing to some degree, and we're less likely to hear language or ideas that create discomfort. Studies have shown that people will tend to ignore new information that challenges important decisions or preconceptions. If you want to make sure your lover gets your point, it must be simple and specific, and it has to be *the* main point. It can't be cluttered up with other complaints and criticisms, because your partner's Reptilian Brain won't be able to carefully select it out and attend to it.

Don't Fill in the Blanks, and Don't Make Your Partner Fill Them in Either

The human brain doesn't deal well with loose ends. When faced with inadequate information, particularly in an emotionally charged situation, we tend to fill in the blanks, in ways based on our own needs, history, fears, and prejudices. If you say no to your partner and she's disappointed, *and* she already has some concerns about herself and the relationship, she will likely fill in the blanks negatively and assume you don't love her or that other things are more important to you than she is.

Our brains generally don't tolerate unsolved or incomplete stories. Very often the things that you simply cannot shake from your mind are unsolved riddles, or behaviors by others that seem incomprehensible. Advertisers have known this for many years. (They've known many things about human behavior for many years.) One way to make a product memorable is to put something in the name or presentation of the product that is an anomaly, something that's unusual or that doesn't fit. The backward *R* in Toys "R" Us is a well-known example of this. Have you noticed that the advertisements, songs, television shows, or other events that you remember longest are often not the best, but rather the most puzzling or annoying?

The human brain attempts to resolve questions at a "mindless," automatic level using information already available: it fills in the blanks in a problem or figure in such a way as to offer rational explanations and allow us to move on. When we smell smoke, we don't need to look in a manual to be warned that danger is near. At a more mundane level, consider the image here. What is it?

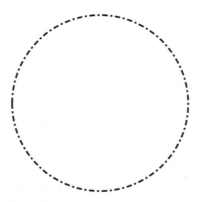

You immediately recognized this as a circle. But a circle is generally a continuous line that closes on itself. If your brain didn't automatically fill in the spaces and assess this pattern, the drawing would remain merely a bunch of dots and dashes.

When faced with a traumatic question—a question with the power to damage us or our feelings of safety—we're most likely to use data from our most primitive, deeply felt doubts and fears. When a partner lies to us, cheats on us, insults or ignores us, our first interpretations of the traumatic question may spring from any old doubts we have ever entertained about ourselves.

The point is, you don't want to make your partner guess what you're thinking or feeling, because *he or she will guess wrong*. If your partner asks, "Why won't you go to the party with me tomorrow night?" and you say, "Because I don't want to!" he might think all kinds of things—that you don't love him, that you're embarrassed to be seen with him, that you don't trust him around other women. What if you replied instead, "I'm really angry with you right now, and I don't want to talk about going out tomorrow night. I need some time to settle down. I'll talk to you later about this when I've calmed down." This response may be brief and relatively negative, but it allows your partner to hold off on filling in the blanks. You've informed him that you're going to come back to him and that there's no urgency for him to do anything immediately. It may be just enough information to help him calm down, even though he may still worry a bit.

UNSPEAKABLE SUBJECTS

Now you're ready for a type of midterm exam. (There are no final exams in relationship work.) Most couples have a subject or two, or many subjects, about which they simply cannot talk. These issues are really taboo. They both know that every time they try, the discussion goes badly. Perhaps they take turns bringing it up and avoiding it or diverting the other's attention. The goal of this "exam" is to practice the organizing skills you have learned throughout this book and bring them to bear on your "unspeakable subjects."

Take about ten minutes to answer the questions that follow. Then take five minutes to share your responses with your partner, without interruption, and to answer any *clarifying* questions the partner might have. Such clarifying questions are meant only to make sure that you got your points across and were understood, not to challenge or defend in any way. Then your partner has five minutes to share his or her subject.

The listed items are not meant to limit you in any way. They're the kinds of questions that I've found helpful in encouraging couples to refine their thinking about problem areas.

1. Briefly describe the subject of disagreement.

2. What typically happens when one of you mentions this subject? What do you fear will happen if you bring it up?

3. On what points do you already agree? (It's helpful to remember that you do already have some positive agreement on the subject.)

4. How do you end up feeling when you try to discuss this?

5. How do you think your partner feels when you try to discuss this? (Asking questions about feelings often encourages empathy, which is often missing in this kind of discussion.)

6. What do you need right now to help you move a little further with this subject? What would feel reassuring?

7. What kind of an outcome do you need? What would seem like a success to you?

8. What do you suppose makes this particular subject difficult to explore? (Ask yourself this question now that you are out of your Reptilian Brain and can think about this issue in a calm, rational manner.)

It's been my experience that couples can accomplish amazing things in just a few minutes when they can access their big brains, get beneath the surface, and discover the common needs and fears that underlie their conflicts. You may wish to make this exercise one of your thirty-minute meetings. Try giving the entire session over to one subject. Describe your subject in about five minutes and then take another five minutes to answering clarifying questions. For the next ten minutes, discuss the subject in the most businesslike fashion you can muster, with the questions and your mutual goals in mind. Then, for ten more minutes, review and plan. How did the discussion go for you? Did either or both of you feel you made progress? Do either of you have more questions that you need answered? What are the next steps? More than likely, you'll need to schedule another partnership meeting on this same subject. Practice! The usual sense of hopelessness that accompanies unspeakable subjects will dissolve as you organize your thoughts and invite your neocortex out to play.

As you practice the techniques introduced in this chapter, you'll become much better prepared to be curious about each other and to ask the right questions, rather than simply defend against feeling helpless, hopeless, and overwhelmed. When you see that your tough problems are manageable once you reveal their real origins, and the needs that drive them, you will very likely notice your heart rate slowing down, your breath coming more easily, and your thinking becoming more creative. You're now able to advance to the most desirable and challenging subjects in every relationship: increasing your sense of closeness and connectedness with each other and developing intimacy.

6

Step Four

Add Positives and Build Intimacy

. . . and then I asked him with my eyes to ask again
yes and then he asked me would I yes to say yes my
mountain flower and first I put my arms around him
yes and drew him down to me so he could feel my
breasts all perfume yes and his heart was going like
mad and yes I said yes I will Yes.

James Joyce, Ulysses (1922)

The work you did in Chapter Five helped you break through some defensive reptilian barriers you and your partner put up to keep yourselves from getting hurt. Now that you have a better understanding of the deeper issues affecting your relationship, you should be able to face them head-on, right?

Not so fast.

When it comes to what we perceive as self-preservation, we are masters at finding ways to defend ourselves. The Reptilian Brain is not so easily tamed and is in many ways ruled by habit—the instinctive habit of saying no.

As important as it is to clarify issues and learn to deal with them, it's equally important to learn to say yes, to introduce as many positives into your relationship as possible. This requires you to be curious about your partner's wants and needs and to be willing to take risks in asking for what you want.

Does this mean meekly submitting to any opinions or danger-ous behaviors your partner wishes to foist on you? Not necessarily. It does mean that by negotiating goals, you can learn to set limits while rebuilding a good relationship. This chapter is about learning to treat your partner well and, within your limits, give each other wonderful things. It's also about learning to ask for what you need and expecting to be treated well.

Each *no* to a partner is, by definition, a rejection. Rejection raises anxiety. The more often we reject, the more distant we become. Often the problem is that saying no is not accompanied by further information. If you ask your partner about going out to a movie and he or she simply says no, what is the message? That depends entirely on the relationship. If all is well and you feel good about yourself and your partner, you don't feel rejected; you just accept that your partner doesn't want to see a movie. But if all is not well, that no might convey a much more negative message. It might suggest, for instance, "Tonight, like most other nights, I really don't want to be with you at the movies or any other place. In fact, I'd rather not be seen in public with you because I'm ashamed of being associated with you." Did your partner really intend to say all that? Maybe, maybe not. But perhaps that's what you heard, and we know by now that what is heard is often much more important than what is actually said.

So how can we avoid being negative and appearing to reject our partners? How can we both give and receive more freely on all lev-els of intimacy?

THE ART AND SCIENCE OF GETTING TO YES

Why is it so difficult to ask someone you love for good things, for things you want or need? Remember, in a reptilian state of feeling angry or fearful, you'll be reluctant to make your needs known. Any suggestion that you're needy or vulnerable will feel as though you're exposing your carotid artery to an attacking beast. It will feel as though you're surrendering all advantage. Instead, you go on the attack with name-calling, nagging, insults, or any number of dirty fighting approaches. This doesn't give your partner any idea about what you want, but instead shuts him or her down to you. Even if a behavior were to improve somewhat after such an attack, the underlying damage to the partnership would remain, and additional repairs would be required.

Stop Setting Yourself Up for No

Often, because of recent events, family history, or previous relationships, we simply don't expect positive, loving words or actions from each other. Maybe we even doubt that we deserve them. Fearful of being rejected or disappointed, we don't even give our partner the opportunity to hear the request. Instead we say to ourselves, "My partner doesn't care enough about me to grant me this small favor"; we've developed a story about being ignored or rejected before we've even asked the question, setting up a self-fulfilling prophecy. We also tend to weave together other stories of neglect until, with little or no evidence, we resent the partner completely for his or her uncaring ways.

Sometimes the way we ask for something actually brings about a negative answer. You might ask in a way that doesn't really tell the partner what he needs to do to please you. Suppose you say, "We never do anything together anymore. Let's go to a movie tonight." What you might really mean is, "I miss going out on dates the way we used to. I wish you would 'ask me out' every once in a while." You may be imagining (as we discussed in Chapter Two) that if he really cared, he would know what you were really asking or be able to read between the lines. Instead, by saying "We never do anything together anymore," you've set yourself up for a negative response by starting your request with a reptilian accusation.

Ask for What You Want

As you proceed, challenge yourself to think of new ways to ask for the things you want. This will require you to ignore old disappointments and fears of being rejected. If you and your partner are now going to try to have a new kind of relationship, then what happened last year or even last week may not be important. If your partner would have smirked a month ago when asked to spend some time cuddling with you, you must now assume that he's willing to offer more and that he really wants to even if he messes it up at first. Of course, if you do experience rejection or injury when asking for or offering more, then you must back up and examine what's getting in the way.

Let's suppose that you've often challenged your partner about not spending time together by saying, "You never want to do anything with me." This time, try sticking to the most minimal statement of your request: "I would like to go out with you. When do you think we could plan this?" If he comes back with excuses about why it's impossible to go out, again stick to basic, simple questions: "Do you want to spend time with me? Can you think of any way we could accomplish this?" You're still asking for what you want, but without accusations or threats. You're asking the most basic negotiation question: Is it important to your partner to have time with you? You can then proceed to figuring out how to accomplish this. It will take some practice, because when we expect disappointment or harm, our Reptilian Brains tend to go on the attack, often with *always* and *never* statements, which will set up counterattack instead of cooperation.

Keep in mind that this is the first day of the rest of your life. I know it's a phrase that can make us squirm, but it's critical to this step. In an effort to bring your relationship to a new place, you're now trying to ask for and offer more than you probably thought was possible. Old stories about feeling rejected when you've asked for something or when you've offered something good are just that— old stories. They give you nothing of value now. You need to assume that your interactions can be better; hence, this is the first day. Use this or a similar mantra to remind yourself that "there is no future in the past."

Evolutionary Tip
The Wish List

You need to give your partner clear information about how to treat you well. The two of you may be a little out of practice, so here's an exercise that may help. Write down a list of five things you would like from your partner, and have your partner do the same for you. You should be able to do each of these in a short amount of time. (In other words, "Build a new addition to the house" would not be appropriate for this list.)

A longer list won't work because then it seems like a list of complaints; five items places responsibility on each of you to think about the list and make a selection (and leaves room for a little surprise). If you name just one thing that you want, your partner may obey but feel somewhat robotic doing it. I encourage you to include only one sexual wish, but others may be physical. For example, you might list the following: (1) Do the dishes one night; (2) Give me a back rub without being asked; (3) Offer me a sexual treat and plan out how to do it; (4) Write me a little love note, like you used to; (5) Take the kids out for two hours on Sunday morning and give me some time to myself.

Once a week, each of you should fulfill one wish from your partner's list. This little effort to reconnect lets the two of you know that you are both working on the relationship and taking it seriously. Remember, this is an experiment. You can revise this list as often as you wish. As you learn about each other, your list might take on new directions.

Keep It Simple

Often couples get into trouble because they make things too complicated. They attempt to interpret each other's behavior or diagnose each other. You need to be as clear as possible about what you actually want in a given situation.

Let's take a difficult example. Jim jumps to his feet or even pushes Lisa when he becomes reptilian. If Jim were in therapy, it might be useful to look at what has happened in his life that causes him to act this way and to theorize as to what he really needs when he pushes Lisa. Lisa might be tempted to analyze Jim's behavior and to tell him that he has an anger problem. She might suggest that he suffers from insecurity or anxiety and that his anger is actually displaced rage at his mother. Naturally, he will not be able to hear any of this.

Isn't what Lisa needs really very simple? She needs Jim to stop pushing her. In fact, until this behavior ceases there's no hope for improvement in their relationship. We can assume that if Jim cannot or will not stop intimidating and pushing Lisa, their relationship will continue to worsen. He has to stop.

So at this point it's not useful to interpret Jim's behavior. Lisa needs to demand that Jim no longer intimidate, push, or assault her in any way, and she must be prepared to follow through by leaving him or calling the police if he's unwilling to meet this demand. I won't work with a couple in which an abuser isn't committed to stop all acts of violence and intimidation or the victim isn't willing to call the police if this commitment is broken.

When emotions get in the way, we complicate simple requests and confuse each other. Remember the work you accomplished in Chapter Five on clarifying your needs? Keep your requests in difficult situations as simple and clear as possible and then build from there.

Refine Your Ideas of a "Good Relationship"

If you don't know what you want when you set out to improve your relationship, you'll have a hard time getting what you need. One way to increase this self-knowledge is to make a fantasy list that can stretch your concept of a good relationship and try out some new ideas. Be as playful as you like. As you design your ideal relationship, dream big and expand your fantasies beyond what you think your partner will or won't do. Too often we develop stories about each other that overly restrict what we expect and hope for (see Chapter Three). These stories then put an end to the adventure of exploring each other. How often have you heard someone complain that his or her ex-lover is now doing things with some new lover that the person "never would have done when we were together?"

The following questions are just a beginning. Add in any other ideas about what you would like to have in your relationship. Once you've completed the list to your satisfaction, discuss your responses with each other. Don't be afraid if you find that your answers don't always match. The goal is not perfect agreement but rather negotiation of good things for both of you. If there are huge differences, there might be underlying issues occurring between you that first require attention. Here goes:

1. How much time should you and your partner spend together? How many days and evenings should you be in the same place? How much time per evening should you spend actually talking to each other or otherwise engaging with each other?

2. What activities should the two of you spend more time doing?

3. How should you have meals together (candlelit, by the TV, going out fast, going out slow and fancy)?

4. How should you and your partner dress around each other (jeans, formal wear, pajamas)?

5. How should you and your partner act around each other (cuddling, joking, distancing, clinging, teasing, casual touching)?

6. How should you greet each other when you wake up and when you meet at the end of your work day or after other separations?

7. How long can you be apart (days, weeks, months), and how should you prepare for longer separations?

8. How should you deal with anger and disappointment?

9. How often should you have sex?

10. How often should you touch each other casually or just caress and cuddle?

11. Is any kind of touch okay, or are there kinds of touch that do not work for you?

12. How should you explore sexuality? How do you wish to discuss or introduce changes in timing, places, or positions in your lovemaking?

13. What would you be doing differently if you were not with your partner?

The last item may be a little controversial, but I believe it to be critical. Whether you admit it or not, a "being single" fantasy has probably crossed your mind, along the lines of, "If I weren't with her, I would spend my life scuba diving in the Bahamas." This fantasy is normal and healthy. It only becomes unhealthy when you actually begin to believe that the only way to change your drab existence is to change the person with whom you live. It rarely works.

> A jealous husband hired a private detective to check on his wife. He insisted that he receive not only a written report but also a video of his wife's movements.
>
> Soon the detective returned with a tape, and they sat down to watch it together. Sure enough, the husband saw his wife meeting a strange man. He saw them laughing together in the park, enjoying lunch at an outdoor café, smiling and holding hands all the while. He saw them go into a club and go dancing and then stop off for coffee, and again they seemed to be thoroughly enjoying themselves. He watched a while longer as other such scenes unfolded.

Suddenly standing up, he said, "I don't believe this!"

"What's not to believe?" asked the detective. "It's right there on the screen."

"I can see that," shouted the husband. "But who knew she could be so much fun?"

Think about what you're missing in life and gauge how important you believe this desire is for you. If it's indeed very important, then by all means set out to obtain that—*with* your partner. Don't use him or her as an excuse for not pursuing your goals. You can't make profound changes in yourself simply by changing your partner.

Define Minimal Helpful Efforts

A journey of a thousand miles begins with but a single step.

Lao-tzu

As you clarify your concerns, wants, and needs, you can better define specific steps toward your goals. At such times, people often think of big changes, but lasting changes are best achieved through small efforts that achieve little successes. Minimal efforts are not to let either of you off from working hard on the issues but instead are to designate safe and relatively manageable behaviors that you can offer each other. These behaviors are demonstrations of good faith, peace offerings, and reassurance that you can relax and develop your relationship.

Suppose your partner says you never seem interested in her. As far as you know, you always listen when she talks, and you bring home small gifts periodically to remind her you care. Your Reptilian Brain is on alert as she explains that she actually needs to be physically touched and that you never seem to want to do that anymore. Now your reptilian responses really kick in; your heart is thumping, and your armpits become moist. The last time you touched her, she said the only thing you were interested in was sex, and that got you pretty angry.

When you ask what would be the minimal effort that could make this better, she says that she loves it when you massage her back and shoulders without being asked. She adds that sometimes this positive feeling has been ruined when you've tried to grope her breast after a moment of rubbing her shoulders. Now you know why she often stiffens when you start to massage her. Together you decide that for the next month, you'll rub her back and shoulders twice a week without touching her in any sexual way, just concentrating on giving her this small pleasure.

Does it sound like you can do this? Do you want to do this? Is anything still in the way? Are you still angry at her? Does the anger need to be addressed before you can do the back rub? And so the questions go. It's often the first small efforts that count the most; remember, even the longest of journeys starts with a single step.

BUILDING AGREEMENT IN A DISTANCED, SHUT-DOWN RELATIONSHIP

In Chapter Two I described distanced, disconnected, silent couples. Such couples may feel particularly overwhelmed because they recognize that even the more simple and easy-to-do interventions in this book require some interaction between them. Each partner in such a shut-down relationship likely fears that he or she is going to be asked to do things that seem impossible.

I've seen a number of partners who accuse the other of not wanting connection, when on further evaluation it appears that both partners play parts in maintaining distance. Because of this ambivalence, partners in a silent struggle often need to be seen in individual therapy first. Their fear of conflict and connection is so strong that when difficult subjects are broached in couples therapy, they both tend to shut down. It's as though they're afraid the therapist is going to place a demand on them that they know they won't be able to meet. Returning to a level of engagement that feels comfortable and satisfying to both seems impossible.

Silent, distant couples need to explore very carefully the nature of their distance and what purpose it serves. Are they so different in their needs that they can't negotiate a supportive relationship? Is one of them fantasizing about a life that in reality would not work for him or her? Is one or both of them depressed? Some couples actually need to begin by dispelling the image they have of how close an "ideal" couple should be. This will prepare them to negotiate more comfortably and build a level of closeness that best fits their respective needs. Are they both willing to try out a few small changes to see if they can be closer?

REPTILES IN LOVE
The Silences of Jack and Diane

Jack and Diane had been together for over twenty years and had two kids, a boy sixteen and a girl of twelve. They were referred by Diane's employee assistance program (EAP) counselor. Diane had been missing deadlines at work and had been irritable with colleagues on several occasions. Her supervisor referred Diane to the EAP out of real concern for her.

The EAP asked her about a recent incident in which she had referred to two colleagues as a "couple of airheads." Diane explained that they were younger women who were always talking about their "happy marriages," which she said as though she were smelling raw sewage.

"Just wait until they see how it really is."

It became clear to the EAP counselor that Diane was unhappy in her marriage. Diane reluctantly agreed, realizing that some form of counseling was necessary if she wanted to keep her job.

When they came in to see me, Jack was clearly uncomfortable and quickly let me know that he thought they were doing fine. This introduction was the most I would hear out of him for some time.

(continued on next page)

(continued)

REPTILES IN LOVE
The Silences of Jack and Diane

Diane noted that her strong reactions at work had convinced her that she could not go on in her marriage—but she didn't want to leave her marriage either.

Talking about their relationship, Jack and Diane described themselves as being fairly shy and not having a lot of friends. They had enjoyed each other's company when they first met, and each had been a little surprised to find someone who seemed to appreciate them. In their infrequent disagreements, one or the other would quickly acquiesce. When there was any disappointment, they just withdrew and stopped talking for a while. The silences became longer and longer.

By the time they came to see me, they couldn't remember the last time they had had sex or even touched each other. They were embarrassed by this and didn't want to talk about it. Neither described any great desire for intimacy, although Diane seemed to believe strongly that a sexless marriage was not right.[1] As Diane talked, she described several other disappointments in the relationship. At no point did Jack attempt to defend or explain himself.

One can imagine that Diane was feeling as though she were the victim of a bait and switch. She started off with a quiet, kind man who seemed genuinely interested in her and ended up with someone who seemed totally uninvolved. Diane was cautious and unsure about relationships from the beginning, and remained puzzled by closeness or affection from anyone but her children. If Jack were to suddenly see the light and become involved, affectionate, and interested, Diane would need to push him away. Similarly, Jack seemed uninvolved, but had panic symptoms when Diane mentioned separation.

As they began to test the waters a bit in terms of what they could do to encourage and soothe the other, and as they reminded each other that they would be satisfied with small changes, they began to seem more at ease. They started having sex again, but both noted that that was not the main improvement for them. Instead, the key thing was that they found that it was okay to ask each other for things and to say no without hurting the other's feelings. They were able to talk about the need for some distance, instead of acting it out and then being hurt, ashamed, and angry. They realized that they both needed short breaks from one another, particularly after they were physically close or had sex. They arrived at what they described as "optimal closeness."

SELF-CONTRACT
FOR CONTINUED GROWTH

As you move toward adding positives and building intimacy in your relationship, you'll probably make a lot of promises to yourself about what you will or will not do from now on. That's a good thing, but we all know where the road paved with good intentions leads. One way to help you solidify the gains you've made and to keep yourself moving forward is to make a contract with yourself.

In the Self-Contract for Continued Growth shown here, check off a couple of tasks that you see as "next steps" for you. Choose items that are achievable so that you don't overwhelm yourself. This contract, like your relationship, should reflect an organic, growing understanding. You may complete a couple of tasks easily over the next thirty days and then return to the contract and assign yourself more. Be proud of such outstanding effort! You may also have a task that takes longer, such as reading a book or learning a new skill with your partner. Give yourselves time and be as playful as possible. You will eventually see results.

SELF-CONTRACT
FOR CONTINUED GROWTH

Within the next thirty days, I would like to continue my relationship work with the following tasks. I will return to this agreement
after that time and reexamine my success and any additional steps
I need to take.

_____ I need to read _____ and/or
_____ (see the Resources or go
browse at your bookstore).

_____ I would like to exchange lists of five wishes each with my
partner.

_____ I will work on improving my own negative stress reactions
in the following ways: _____
_____

_____ I will make an appointment for a physical examination.

_____ I will ask my doctor about _____

_____ I would like to have an evening date each week with my
partner.

_____ I would like to take a minivacation or overnighter each
month with my partner.

_____ I need us to schedule partnership meetings _____ time(s)
per week.

I would propose these days and times for our meeting:
_____

I would like to add these rules to the partnership
meeting: _____
_____
_____

_____ I would like to try some brainstorming on the following
subjects (Generate as many possible options on an issue as

rapidly as possible, initially without criticism or comment. Then go back through the list and evaluate. This technique is a quick way of engaging your neocortex and your humor.): _____

_____ I would like to develop a signal that we can agree means "I love you and I care, but I can't talk right now," or some other positive message:

_____

_____

_____ I would like to make an agreement about how we should return to a subject once we have taken a break.

_____ I would like to have a discussion about how we can safely talk about sex.

_____ I would like for each of us to write the apology to each other that we would like to hear from the other. In this experiment you will each write down what you wish your partner would say to you. This allows you to consider clearly what you are hoping for and will clarify for your partner what you see as the critical points of an apology. An additional step is each of you to read your partner's wished-for apology back. Although it is your words you are hearing, hearing them from your partner may be quite healing and lead to further positive communication about what has happened between you.

_____ I would like to have a meeting about an unspeakable subject and review the details of that problem very specifically, using the form at the end of Chapter Five.

_____ I have a completely different idea of something I would like to offer my partner: In the next _____ days I will _____

_____   _____
Signature   Date

There's something about committing a signature to a piece of paper that pushes us out of the Reptilian Brain and into the neo-cortex. Before making such a commitment, we should assess and organize our thoughts and consider the risks and benefits. The added anxiety of signing the agreement will be offset by the security of knowing what each of you can expect. Reptiles can't make commitments; humans can and should.

Yes, this contract with yourself is important enough to sign. You'll find many temptations to draw away from your goals and begin to ignore your relationship. This is normal. Make every attempt to resist by making your relationship a priority above all other considerations. You owe this to yourself.

Two Steps Forward, One Step Back: Relapse Is Normal

Don't be disappointed if you can't always live up to your contract or if you occasionally break the promises you make to yourself. I've noted, over the years, a kind of rhythm in couples work. Couples will often come in after the third or fourth session and announce success. They report that they're doing more together and speaking more kindly to each other. They'll giggle and mention that they've been able to be more playful with each other, in such a way as to let me know that play has gone far beyond video games and dancing. They begin to ask about termination of treatment and thank me profusely for my help.

This presents a quandary for me. I don't want to seem as though I'm just trying to keep them coming into therapy, yet I know that many of these couples are not really finished. It's very likely that within a short time—probably a week—they'll have a real finger-pointing, neighbor-annoying, cat-scaring fight. It will likely occur over something stupid, as most fights do. The partners will, possibly unconsciously, try out all their old behaviors on each other again. They'll disagree on who did what first, but it really doesn't matter. What matters is that they will be at risk of believing that all their fears about attempting change have proved true.

They may say to each other, "Look at us. Nothing has changed. You're doing the same things you've always done even though you now know how much they hurt me. You know the danger we're in, yet you decide to go back to all that old stuff. I feel just as angry, hurt, and crazy as I did before we ever tried to change anything. Maybe we really don't belong together after all."

The fact is, most people don't even give up old *clothes* without trying them on one more time. We certainly don't give up lifelong habits and personal defenses without trying them out again. They're simply too hard-wired into our primitive brains. Relapse seems to be a normal and perhaps even necessary step in the full change process. So keep in mind that it's unrealistic to believe that you can make a few changes and suddenly clear up all the potential conflict, pain, and bad habits in your lives.

In emergency medical care, the first tasks are to clear the air passages and stop the bleeding. Couples work uses a similar "protocol." Initially, a reasonable goal is to bandage some of the worst injuries and to stop the partners from reinjuring each other. The next step is the healing process, which will take longer.

I hope that the big fight you have in the middle of working on your relationship offers you more hope rather than less. This huge and often disappointing fight, this return to old behaviors you thought you'd left behind, doesn't indicate that your relationship is unworkable. It's usually quite the opposite. It suggests that you're fearful of letting the relationship simply coast or drift back to the old ways. Without further effort on your parts, this is indeed a risk. Such a drift toward old habits or the status quo is normal throughout nature.

The big new fight then is a way of inoculating yourselves against this negative drift. It calls on you to test and push your relationship further. It invites you to examine those subtle ways in which you betray each other. It reminds you that old injuries may still need to be dealt with, grieved over, and repaired. Whether you're in therapy or doing this work on your own, you're now ready to challenge each other in new ways, repeatedly reminding yourself to refuse to harm your partner or to increase your defenses. You now know that it's awfully easy to slip back and that you both must be aware of the warning signs.

However, you now also have new tools at your disposal you never had before. You've probably already had some negotiations that have helped you understand each other. You're adding positives and building what respected author and couples therapist John Gottman refers to as your "emotional bank account."[2] With each success, you're insulating your relationship against the external world and those odd moments when one of you inevitably slips and disappoints the other.

In the next chapter, we're going to discuss using these same skills to build emotional and physical intimacy, which may include sexual intercourse but is also much more than that.

7

Step Five
Learn Nonreptilian Lovemaking

A terrible thing happened again last night—nothing.
Phyllis Diller

Ah, sex, the most hoped for, misunderstood, and feared of intimate relations. In the hope that you won't shy away from this
chapter, I want to make a few quick comments about sexuality.

1. Sex is the most complicated of interpersonal endeavors,
   elegantly combining both primitive and advanced character-
   istics and brain activities.

2. There is no such thing as normal sex.

3. No one can tell anyone else how or how often he or she
   should have sex.

4. Impassioned sexuality is possible with a trusted partner in a
   safe, secure, and loving environment.

5. Sexual difficulties may have many different causes, and most
   are quite treatable when correctly diagnosed.

6. Because intimacy and sex are such anxiety-provoking topics,
   partners are often reluctant to discuss them.

In this chapter, we explore these six concepts and find out how to keep our reptilian impulses from interfering with one of the most basic yet most complex area of our lives—sexuality.

Sex Is the Most Complicated of Interpersonal Endeavors, Elegantly Combining Primitive and Advanced Characteristics and Brain Activities

Sex is the most difficult interaction to discuss. That's probably why there's so much joking about it. But it may be our response to sexuality that most separates us from other species. Sex is complicated in humans. Even in the most casual sexual encounter, in which two partners hardly know each other's names and have little interest in maintaining a relationship, there is an intricate tapestry of needs being met.

Consider the complex web of responses occurring within your sexual experience. In any given sexual act, your reptilian, mammalian, and higher brain responses are performing an elaborate dance as they govern your physical preparation, emotional bonding, communication, creativity, and performance. Because sexuality is a total experience, meaning that it affects and uses every portion of your being, it is also exquisitely sensitive to a wide range of physical, emotional, historical, cultural, and familial influences.

If you have been raised to believe that sexuality is inherently bad or dirty and that sexual needs are embarrassing, then discussing any level of sensuous need may be quite difficult. If you believe that you are an unattractive person, then it may be impossible to view yourself as a sensuous or appealing partner in intimacy. If you typically view sex as full-penetration, howling, toe-curling, sheet-ripping, orgasm-laden intercourse, then you may fail to consider a wide range of other equally sensual and satisfying intimate experiences.

There Is No Such Thing as Normal Sex

> When I'm caught between two evils, I take the one I've never tried.
>
> Mae West

The concept of normality in sex can be extremely damaging. How many of us have been horribly ashamed of such normal activities as masturbation? How many believe that our sex organs are abnormally small, large, unusual, or ugly? Given that we are often preoccupied with our looks, our intelligence, our incomes, and other areas of comparison to our fellow humans, is it any wonder that we also think of our sexual lives in this competitive manner?

Eliminating the concept of normal from sexual language can be enormously freeing. If a wife says that it's normal to have sex once per week, the implication may be that her husband is either wanting too much or providing too little and that consequently there's something wrong with him. Does this make him feel any closer to her? Does he suddenly feel more or less sexually aroused because he now realizes that his wife thinks he's abnormal? Of course not!

If, wanting more sex, she were to say, "Look, I really feel close to you and would like to be more sexual. I'd like to try to have sex more often," he would be much more likely to be responsive.

This isn't foolproof, however. Due to his own anxiety, he may still hear an accusation or insult that she didn't intend, but this anxiety is more workable if the overall message is one of joining and desire.

If wanting less sex, she might say, "I know that you want to have sex more often than I do, but sometimes that doesn't work for me. Can we work something out?"

In this phrasing as well, there's no suggestion that he's wrong for wanting more. Compare such a statement to "What's wrong with you? Are you some kind of animal?"

Although eliminating the concept of normal from sexual language can be liberating, it doesn't imply that *everything* must be okay with you. Sexual behavior that's harmful to any other person (obviously including sex with a child) is not acceptable. There may also be specific sexual behaviors that are unacceptable to you personally. Your reasons for considering these behaviors off-limits are yours alone, and whether you wish to challenge or explore them is completely up to you. This doesn't mean, however, that your partner is defective for finding them desirable or interesting (unless their interests cause harm to you, your partner, or others).

When you and your partner discuss a particular sexual behavior without placing blame or accusing each other of being abnormal, you still may not agree on specific practices. However, it's likely that you'll find you can substitute a wide range of sexual behaviors that meet both your needs and your partner's.

No One Can Tell Anyone Else How or How Often He or She Should Have Sex

Most sexual difficulties couples experience have nothing to do with technique but more with trust, communication, and safety. There's a lot of information available on how to make love. (I've included some of these in the Resources section of this book.) When two people genuinely want to be as close as possible and open up to each other, the mechanics of best positions, times, toys, movies, and other aspects of their intimacy are negotiable.

The primary question between two intimate partners is not whether they have sex or not. It's whether they have sufficient positive feelings between them to want to be good to each other. When such positive feelings are present, sexuality is a natural part of the relationship. When such positive feelings are present, touching each other in pleasant and rewarding ways will be relatively easy and natural, and whether you engage in sexual intercourse or not, will feel like a mutual decision. Without these positive feelings, sexual intercourse is unlikely to be rewarding, and intimacy will continue to deteriorate.

Sex is about feeling good and feeling close. You can neither impose sexual intimacy on your partner nor refuse all such intimacy without affecting the relationship negatively. In any discussion of affection, you must always back up to what is interfering with positive feelings and then work forward to how to best meet each other's needs.

Impassioned Sexuality Is Possible with a Trusted Partner in a Safe, Secure, and Loving Environment

I know, I know: the thrill of new or illicit love can be extraordinarily exciting. There is evidence that such novel experiences stimulate the brain in a different manner than does sex with a longtime partner. It's the novelty of the situation, more than new love, that provides the added oomph to the sexual experience of a new sexual partner. But couples who have a great deal of trust and affection for each other are uniquely positioned to fully give to each other with relaxed, creative, neocortex brains. These couples can push at the boundaries of their affection and overcome their embarrassment and fears while being comforted and protected by each other. They are to be envied.

Because novel experiences do stimulate the mind and body differently from the routine, it's important for couples to reinvigorate and enhance their lovemaking. Again, this doesn't mean that you need to become sexual acrobats or that each experience requires new instruments, toys, or playground equipment. You may, however, want to periodically engage in sex in a slightly different way or in different rooms or cities, or do a little role playing or dress-up in order to simulate newness as well as to maintain that necessary sense of playfulness.

Sexual Difficulties Have Many Different Causes, and Most Are Quite Treatable When Correctly Diagnosed

What's the difference between anxiety and panic?
Anxiety is the first time you can't do it a second time, and
panic is the second time you can't do it the first time.

Most people experience sexual difficulties at some point in their lives. The great tragedy is that most couples don't seek help. If you experience a lack of desire or satisfaction problems you may be embarrassed and fearful of what this means and ask yourself, "Is something wrong with me? Am I getting old? Don't I love my partner?" Often all it means is that some form of stress or anxiety has intruded into the bedroom. Once you've experienced a physical reaction (or nonreaction) to stress, you start to worry that you will experience it again (that is, you won't have an erection, won't feel sexually aroused, or won't have an orgasm). Your anxiety level goes up, and the very part of your brain that's most responsible for sexual arousal, the Reptilian Brain, is suddenly preoccupied with fight-or-flight anxiety responses. What you feared would happen, will happen.

Sexual dysfunction is common in both men and women and is generally treatable. Sexuality is a complex set of responses, and much can go wrong in sexual arousal and performance. Stress, medical conditions, drug side effects, trauma, and relationship concerns can all play a role in disrupting the physical expression of love. The release of such medications as Viagra, Levitra, and Cialis for erectile dysfunction (ED) have given many couples renewed hope and reinvigorated their sex lives. Even more important, these medications (and their advertising campaigns) have increased public awareness and discussion of sexual problems. As more and more couples recognize that this is a common problem, it will, one hopes, allay some of the fear and shame associated with such concerns.

So complex is sexual arousal and response that in many cases, difficulties have neither one source nor one solution. A man experiencing ED may find that Viagra produces a great deal of relief, but if his partner is tense and angry, erections may actually add to that resentment. Some women have felt quite hurt by the idea that their man would need a chemical in order to "tolerate" sex with them. In some older couples, women have said that they were relieved that their husbands were not pursuing them for sex, and that the renewed attention was not welcome.[1]

For all these reasons, any person or couple experiencing sexual dysfunction should have a physical examination and discuss their sexual arousal and satisfaction concerns with their physician. They should also take a close look at their situation in terms of external stressors (for example, job or financial stress) or marital tensions (arguments, avoidance, performance anxiety). It may be that removal of such stressors will alleviate the symptoms of sexual dysfunction. If not, a combined approach of medical interventions and a focus on the relationship may be most effective.

For example, if a partner has been sexually abused, she may find some sexual approaches not only uncomfortable but actually frightening and overwhelming. She may still have tremendous desire to see her partner happy and to feel close to him. This is very workable if both are willing to respectfully look into a variety of ways to be close. He may have to remember that he needs to approach her gently and speak to her softly when he wants to be intimate, or that he should not initially touch her body in specific places. She may find that some forms of relaxation techniques, or sensuous massage, can enable her to move into passion more safely. Together they can test the boundaries of their sexual relationship and then see whether those boundaries can be expanded through cooperative discussion and exploration.

REPTILES IN LOVE

Easy to Be Hard

Finally Bob and Carol admitted somewhat late in treatment to the problems they were having with their sexual encounters. Bob had had several experiences of not being able to develop a full erection or of losing his erection during intercourse. Carol was gentle and understanding at times, and at other times became suddenly angry. Lately, each time they attempted to make love, Bob began the frustrated man's silent prayer: "I hope it works. I hope it works. I hope it works." He could feel the tension building in himself and was

(continued on next page)

(continued)

REPTILES IN LOVE
Easy to Be Hard

considering the use of Viagra. Carol felt that his sexual problems were due to her weight gain or because he wanted someone younger or was angry at her for some reason.[2]

When they began to talk about their lovemaking and how aware they were of each other's moods, they were able to see that if she momentarily became distracted, he instantly felt rejected. She would generally try to cover up these little lapses rather than admit that she had lost interest for a second. At other times, it was he who became distracted by overwhelming thoughts about troubles at his office. As his erection softened, he would become increasingly desperate, trying to ignore what was happening with wild, futile thrusting.

If Bob suddenly thinks about the office and becomes distracted, does this mean that he no longer cares for Carol? He could easily just say, "Wow, I just suddenly focused on that problem at the office for a second and got totally distracted. Can we just take a moment and try again a little later?" For a connected couple, unless they're simply too tired and can't get back into the mood, there's every likelihood that they'll be able to rejoin each other sexually after this minor distraction. Certainly there is less danger than if he keeps trying to make something happen and refuses to give Carol information as to what the problem is. It's no wonder that her Reptilian Brain experiences rejection and leads her to blame herself because she's too fat. People always do better with information and guidance about their partner's needs and problems.

Many busy couples tend to give lovemaking a very low priority. As they become more uncertain and uncomfortable with intimacy, they may attempt "quick" sex on Friday night, when they're both exhausted and really want to get some rest. All their fears of this not being a successful experience are then compounded by a time crunch. The luxury of recovering from a lost erection or other distraction is simply not available to them, so they roll over and go to sleep, disappointed.

In most cases of sexual problems, the goal of treatment is not to learn new sexual behaviors or to retrain yourself as if you were a sexual beginner. The goal is simply to find expedient ways for you and your partner to help each other relax, slow your heart rate, calm your brain, and reinvolve yourselves with each other in a playful, affectionate manner.

Because Intimacy and Sex Are Such Anxiety-Provoking Topics, Partners Are Often Reluctant to Discuss Them

Due to the intensity of feelings surrounding the sexual experience, couples will often resist exploring sexual concerns even, or especially, with each other. Reptilian defenses run rampant.

Men experiencing ED will often avoid discussion, hide from their partner, or even become angry when the topic of sex is introduced. Women experiencing decreased interest in sex may tell themselves and their partners that it's just normal and there's nothing that can be done about it. As the other partner becomes more frustrated with the lack of physical intimacy, the couple may avoid discussion of the problem entirely (flight), or such discussions may become more angry and aggressive (fight). At the very time that you're trying to discuss getting closer, you're more likely to push each other further away with judgmental, blaming, and defensive language. Changing this language will change your relationship and your sexual experience.

REPTILES IN LOVE
Show Me That You Love Me

Tony and Tina had worked hard on their relationship and had resolved their problems surrounding finances, discipline of the children, and household chores. They remarked on how well they were getting along and then both seemed to grow quiet at the same moment. We had done good work together, and their relationship was better, but both stumbled and stammered as they approached the unspeakable.

It was Tina who broke the silence. "Tony's not happy with our love life. He's always complaining that we never make love. Even if we do have sex, he still says that he doesn't think I'm all that interested. I really like being with him, but when anything about sex comes up, it's just such a turnoff."

As Tina spoke, Tony was clearly uncomfortable and began to look angry. "Sure we've had sex lately, but it still seems like she's just putting up with my wishes. She's never once taken the initiative. I always ask and then when she gives in, we usually end up having a pretty good time. Is it too much to ask that she would now and then show some interest in me?"

Tony and Tina were now talking about the most delicate of their issues. Tina was angry that Tony would act as though they never had sex, when in fact she felt that she was pretty responsive to him when he asked. Tony had been stewing for years at what he perceived as Tina's lack of interest in him.

Tina felt that Tony was increasingly treating her like a piece of meat. The romantic ways with which he had once courted her were largely gone. Tony accused Tina of not being interested in sex, but he didn't tell her that he wanted to be pursued once in a while. He claimed, "I would give anything to be treated like a sex object just once!"

It's not a secret that women are stimulated differently than men. It's often been noted that men can become spontaneously aroused by a picture, fantasy, image, or attractive person, whereas many women need more time to warm up to sexual feelings with additional stimuli, such as talking, holding, and touching. Many women therefore will be quite responsive to affection, and this can then turn into a sexual experience. But the guy who is waiting for his partner to suddenly announce, "God almighty, am I ever horny!" may be waiting a long time.

Gradually, Tina gave more details about what she found to be pleasant and erotic, and Tony encouraged her to try to show him some spontaneous affection when she felt like it, whether it led to sex or not. Tina worried about sending the wrong message if she didn't want sex. She didn't want to find herself in the position of having to say no and start the old battle all over again. With this information, Tony and Tina began talking about how to show affection without drifting into battle. This was a very good start, alleviating a lot of useless fears about whether they were really attracted to each other.

WORKING ON SEXUAL INTIMACY

The six concepts we just highlighted are obviously the tip of the sexual iceberg. Some of them may apply to you, and others may not. No matter which of these issues apply to your relationship, the only way to resolve the conflicts you're having with your sexual partner is through nonreptilian communication.

Before you can talk about sex, however, you need to agree to some guidelines. Most discussions of sexual intimacy, in therapy or in the popular press, seem to be aimed at pushing partners toward each other. What if this isn't the issue? What if you truly want to be close, but some form of anxiety or fear is blocking this? What follows are some tips for looking at your sexual relationship in a safe fashion (many of which are similar to the ones you've read about in earlier chapters concerning other relationship issues):

1. **The first discussion should probably *not* occur in the bedroom.** If there has been tension between you in the bedroom, then move to a different room to ease this tension. The discussion may be easier if you're at the dining room table with notepads in front of you, much like other discussions described in this book. Give yourself every possibility to relax and feel safe for this meeting. In later discussions, as you begin to feel closer to each other and want to talk more about the mechanics of sex, then you may want to move this discussion back into the bedroom or to a sofa where you can touch each other while you talk.

2. **List the things that will make it most possible for you to relax during a discussion of sex.** You may not want your partner to sit too close initially, or you might like to hold hands while you talk. You may not want your partner to use sexualized or obscene language. ("Talking dirty" may be stimulating during foreplay but offputting during this discussion about closeness.)

3. **Agree on a time limit and a way to end the discussion if it starts to go poorly.** Take a moment now and think about a time when you've tried to have a discussion about some aspect of your sexual relationship and it went poorly. What happened? Did the two of you begin to assign blame or to question each other's motivations or sexual powers? Did you discuss your sexual concerns not as a solvable problem you both faced but as a failing of one or both of you? Did one of you suggest that the other should get help? These are all evidence of the Reptilian Brain kicking in. Such behaviors would suggest that the discussion was going too long or was too intense. As described in Chapter Four, you'll benefit from having

time limits on your discussion of intimacy and ways of taking breaks when you experience the fight-or-flight warning symptoms.

4. **Now that you've picked the time and place for discussion, is there anything else that gets in the way of improving your sexual experience?** Are there any other problems that keep you from having a cooperative discussion about enjoying each other? Are there issues that must be addressed before you can increase your closeness? For example, if you have some unresolved betrayal on your mind, the last thing you want to think about is sex. This doesn't mean that every vestige of such a betrayal will need to be forgotten before you can enjoy sex again. It does mean, however, that you may need some reassurance and protections, such as evidence of your partner's firm commitment to you as discussed in Chapter Eight, in order to explore sexuality safely.

Taking past behaviors into consideration, do you need any rules for this discussion? For example, should you agree not to bring up each other's families in any way while meeting about intimacy? Are visual aids okay or needed for this particular interaction? Are there any other limits on this discussion? If there are unresolved subjects that get in the way, would an agreement that you will return to these at a later meeting help, or do you need to address them first?

5. **Define what you see as improvement.** Let's say you're becoming increasingly comfortable with closeness. The problems or resentments that kept you apart are diminishing, and you both see better things ahead; however, your relationship history hasn't always been great, and there are negative memories competing with your reawakened desires. What's been missing in your relationship? What would tell you that you are loved? What fantasies do you want to have fulfilled in this redefined relationship?

Again take notes on all these questions and add anything else you think would add to your love life. As you prepare to share them with your lover, try to be very specific.

REPTILES IN LOVE
A Bad Night in Waukesha

Mary and Jeff decided that the coming Friday would be their night for romance. They shipped the kids out to a neighbor and prepared for their big night. They each thought about how to make this evening really special and envisioned beautiful scenes with one another. On Friday, Mary arrived home from work first and began to prepare a really lovely meal. She brought out scented candles and selected mood music. Jeff stopped on the way home for flowers and then stopped again and picked up some items at the local adults-only store. Mary showered, dressed, and made herself up more carefully than she had done in a long time. She worked on the final preparations for her fancy dinner.

As Jeff came in he presented his flowers, a bottle of wine, and a pizza he had picked up on the way home. He leered at Mary and exclaimed at how beautiful she looked. He promptly announced that while he took a shower, Mary should check out the surprises in the bag and then meet him in the bedroom naked—and disappeared into the bathroom before she could reply. Mary began to seethe as she grabbed the surprise bag and removed a pornographic movie, some sex toys, and a Richard Nixon mask. This was not at all what she had in mind for a romantic evening. She told Jeff what he could do with his pizza and had some other colorful suggestions as well.

Jeff couldn't believe what was happening. He thought she would get a kick out of the Nixon mask. This episode just served to remind him not only that the romance was gone but that Mary had completely lost her sense of humor.

Both Jeff and Mary had the best of intentions. Their idea of spending a romantic evening together was a great one, and they were pleased that they had agreed to it. The trouble with their plan was the same as in many relationships: Jeff and Mary thought they were speaking a common language when they decided to have a "romantic evening." Their mistake was in their failure to define romance for each other. They both had ideas of what that would entail, and with a little discussion, they both could have had what they wanted.

Jeff thought that all the suggestive smiles and comments about their romantic evening meant that they would rewrite the book on sex, the way they used to—before kids. Mary envisioned the evening more like a date with a romantic dinner, likely leading to sex. She expected to be wooed. Her expectations were dashed when Jeff came home, never noticed that she had prepared dinner, and immediately told her to get undressed. When she told Jeff this, he said it made him feel as though he were some kind of rapist. They had gone quickly from an exciting attempt at reviving their marriage to having thoughts that the marriage might be beyond salvation, when a short discussion before their "date" could have prevented all this anger and hurt.

6. **Expand the discussion between the two of you by asking the tough questions:**

- Are there any old issues that really get in the way of our lovemaking? What do we need to do to lessen the tension around these issues?

- Do either of us have any current problems that get in the way of our lovemaking (job stress, financial stress, physical problems)? How might we lessen the tension around these issues? Can we help each other?

- What do each of us want more or less of in our lovemaking? More foreplay? More time spent together

before we go to bed? More experimentation? Oral sex?
More time cuddling after sex?

- How can we evaluate our experiences?

- How do we explore sexuality when we haven't really
done much of this before?

- How do we negotiate the differences in what each of
us wants?

Rarely are two people so completely sexually compatible that
they both like exactly the same things. Clearly there will be differences in your sexual likes and dislikes. Once again it will be helpful to stay away from judgmental language. If you heard the
following responses from your partner, which one would allow you
to keep talking to him:

"That's disgusting. If you think you'd enjoy that, then you must
be sick," or "I'm really not as interested in that as you are. Is there
something else we could try that might work just as well for you?"

Everything you do to improve your relationship is an experiment, and not every plan will turn out to be successful. You should
be willing to talk about what happens without blaming or accusing.
Being able to make corrections on the path to intimacy is critical
and will prepare you for a lot more enjoyment.

AIDS TO THE SEXUAL DISCUSSION

Assuming that you have established a degree of closeness that allows
for playful discussion of sex, you now open a door to tremendous
opportunity. In addition to your own fantasies and sexual dreams, a
wide range of books, films, educational programming, and sexual
aids are available. If you visit the relationships section of your local
bookstore, you might be surprised at the number and range of books
on sexuality.[3] These can be extremely helpful.

Books and videos that are used purely for sexual stimulation should be chosen carefully to match your mutual interests and mood at the time. This too may require some experimentation. Men tend to be visually stimulated, whereas women may be more stimulated by a good romantic story line. Some partners may be aroused by pornography with no story at all. There is such a wide range of material available that with communication and experimentation, the two of you are sure to find something mutually enjoyable.

Educational materials on sexuality can be quite stimulating in themselves. Most of us labor under some pretty harmful misconceptions about our bodies, our partners, and sexuality, and can benefit from a little education. Such references also place challenges and fantasies outside the relationship. Looking at a book or a video can be less anxiety provoking for you and your partner than trying to produce verbal descriptions of what you want. Pointing at a passage or a picture in a book and saying "I'd really like to try that" may be much easier than trying to describe or ask for that behavior on your own. That this behavior is in a book is also a reminder that you're not alone in the world. More important, there is less rejection in disagreement. If your partner looks at the picture you've indicated and declines, it will feel less personal. He's rejecting an image from an outsider rather than an idea or wish of yours.

Once Again, Be Specific

The human body is an extraordinary piece of work. We all have the same equipment that functions in the same ways. At the same time, each body is individual enough that touching a spot one inch to the left of the navel may feel sensually arousing to one person, produce no reaction in another, and actually annoy a third. Sex can become better and better as you learn more and more about each other's bodies (the kind of intimate knowledge that's not available in casual relationships).

As you begin to explore each other's bodies, you might want to give feedback as to what feels good. You may find that touch, even on parts of your body that are very close together, produces widely varying responses. One feedback method is to rate touch on a scale. You don't have to be exact about this. Remember it's for pleasure and feedback, not science.

Touch Rating Scale

+3	The best feeling ever.
+2	That's really good. Go back to that a lot.
+1	That's nice.
0	Neutral.
−1	That's kind of annoying.
−2	That really bothers me. You probably shouldn't do that.
−3	That hurts. Don't ever do that again!

This rating scale allows you to give quick feedback with minimal thought. (It can be helpful in moments of arousal not to have to think about words and sentences.) With such specific guidance, your partner may gradually develop ways to play with your body and maximize your pleasure. And remember, your ratings of physical experience or sensation may change over time, so keep exploring!

Don't Forget to Touch Each Other

The warmth and comfort of physical contact, including sexuality, is healing and important to human beings. Partners need to have comfort with and attraction for each other, including a means of negotiating their closeness. You should strive to create as many opportunities for positive contact as possible, in your preferred manner, even when intercourse is not desirable or possible.

Sexuality is a challenging subject for many couples, but such discussion can produce wonderful experiences if approached in a nonreptilian state. Planned, specific, safe, and respectful discussion of wants, needs, and fears will allow you to explore each other and gently push the boundaries of your intimate experiences. Giving each other information and absolutely avoiding personal attack will increase your closeness and develop levels of intimacy that you may not have considered possible.

––––––––––

You have now "completed" the five steps to improving your relationship. Of course, they're never really completed; they move, change, and grow as your relationship evolves. As time goes on, you may want to review those steps that worked well for you, as well as those that didn't. Keep the experiment going!

The next part of this book explores some special issues that many couples face: surviving betrayal, entering couples therapy, and, finally, facing the reality that you and your partner may be better off apart.

Part III

Special Issues for Evolving Reptiles

Once Bitten . . .

Surviving Betrayal

Pat lay on his deathbed. His wife Wanda sat near him, and he beckoned her closer. "Wanda, my dear, there's something I must confess."

Wanda hushed him, "Save your strength. Don't try to talk."

"No, Wanda," he said. "I want to die with a clear conscience. I need to confess that I was unfaithful to you."

"I know, Love," she replied. "Why else would I have poisoned you?"

How does one survive and work through a major betrayal? In this chapter I'd like to review a broad range of betrayals, from what is for many the most severe—the affair—through more moderate betrayals, such as role changes, not living up to promises, and choosing family over mates. Many people tell me that the injury such betrayals inflict makes them feel as if their most precious childhood dreams were destroyed, once and for all. Obviously this subject is more complex than can be adequately addressed in one chapter but I'd like to offer some pointers and additional resources, to help you think about preventing betrayal or to get started in your recovery.

Betrayals, whether small or profound, create a crisis because you never again see your partner the same as you did before. The more severe the betrayal the more likely it is to demolish your faith in your partner. Such betrayals can also raise questions about yourself that you have never considered needing to answer, such as "Am I safe with my partner?" "Was she only pretending to love me?" "Am I such a loser that the person I love can't love me?" After a major betrayal, everything is different. The following list of betrayals is ranked from the most severe to "lesser" betrayals, although you may weigh these experiences somewhat differently.

1. My partner's having an affair.

2. There's nothing going on; we're just friends.

3. My partner hit me.

4. My partner misused our money.

5. My family comes first.

6. My needs have changed.

7. Our roles have changed.

My Partner's Having an Affair

As you can imagine, this is the harshest and most traumatic type of betrayal for many couples and therefore deserves special attention. If you want more information about preventing and recovering from affairs, two of the best references are Not "Just Friends," by Shirley Glass, and Private Lies, by Frank Pittman (see the Resources). I urge couples who have experienced this kind of betrayal to seek counseling, read books, and use any other supports available because of the drastic reptilian responses they will almost certainly experience.

Throughout this book we have discussed the Reptilian Brain's response to perceived threat. What can be more threatening than betrayal by your loved one? During such a crisis, you can expect to experience rushes of fear, anger, and hurt, and with them you will experience the full range of reptilian responses. You'll find your short-term memory affected, as well as your ability to concentrate and organize your thoughts. You may have sudden thoughts of running away or even of hurting your partner. It will be difficult to see anything from your partner's perspective, both for the obvious reasons and because of the neurological changes you are experiencing. At such times, people feel extraordinarily confused, and many report, "I feel like I'm going crazy."

Along with the affair comes the emotional experience of discovering that sainthood stories about your true love are inaccurate. These are profound betrayals, potentially fatal to the relationship; betrayals that challenge or irrevocably alter one or both partners' views of the other.

But when partners decide to stay together after a serious betrayal, they've made an important yet tenuous contract. This is the paradox. We all tend to defend ourselves and attempt to justify, to ourselves and others, our most outlandish behaviors. No one whom I know suddenly decides, "Today I'll do something stupid, self-destructive, and harmful to my partner." There must be some explanation or rationale for the behavior, and this needs to be understood and explained. If the betrayer attempts to explain, however, it will sound as if he feels that his behavior was not so bad, or even that it was his partner's fault. Even in the best explanation or apology, the betrayed partner may hear the message that she has no right to feel so hurt or be so angry. This is very dangerous territory indeed.

If partners want to recover from betrayal, they need to go through a series of steps that will ultimately allow them to reestablish their bond:

1. The unfaithful partner must acknowledge that she committed harm. She doesn't need to admit that she's a harmful or dangerous or stupid person, but simply that her action has caused injury. The nature of the harm will need to be described in detail, because in affairs, there is always the compounding

betrayal of lies and deception. The details of this step are not about the actual behaviors during the affair, but recognizing how the betrayal has impacted the partner.

In addition to recognizing the harm she's done, the perpetrator of the affair must decide whether she sees it as wrong or not. If she decides that the affair was not wrong or that it was justified, she'll be in a poor position to reassure her partner that it won't happen again. In fact, he can only anticipate that it *will* happen again.

2. The offending partner must agree to completely discontinue all association with the affair partner and to offer some assurance of her partner's safety from harm. This also has to be a detailed agreement, including any possible exceptions to a no-contact rule, such as if the affair were with a neighbor. In an affair with a colleague, what are the new rules surrounding any further contact with that colleague? What if there is absolutely no way to completely avoid the colleague? In such a case the firm commitment must be that any contact is kept strictly to business.

3. Both partners have to commit to working on the relationship. The nature of this commitment also requires careful description so that both partners know what is expected of them and how they will measure their improvement, their chances of staying together, and their emotional growth.

4. The partners will need to discuss the details of the offense. This is difficult, but if such details, including when, how, where, and why, are not disclosed, the secrecy and the resulting fantasies surrounding it will continue to haunt the relationship. As mentioned in point 1, because deception is inherent to affairs and many other betrayals, the offended partner will need to see clear evidence of honest disclosure.

In an affair you require information and you must ask many questions and insist on knowing the details. This accomplishes several critical tasks. It maintains contact between you and ensures that the affair is not swept under the rug. It also elicits a commitment from your partner to fully join you and stop protecting the affair and the affair partner. Finally, it challenges you to have the hardest discussion you'll probably ever have—a challenge that will very likely enhance your relationship. Try to recognize, however, when the questions no longer seem to serve a purpose. It may be at that point that you need something else from your partner, a ritual, a return to dating or other commitments, in order to feel safe and in control of your life again.

5. The unfaithful partner should also admit regret and apologize. Some partners who have committed such a betrayal forget or avoid this step. They feel they have explained themselves and committed to staying and being faithful, but actually neglect the critical step of apologizing. The apology needs also to be in a form that fits the offended partner's needs. Sometimes an initial apology is made in a flip, off-the-cuff, or even angry fashion that doesn't help at all.

These steps can occur in any order and may be repeated. In other words, reviewing the details of an affair (or of other offenses to be discussed later) once will not necessarily offer you or your partner sufficient relief from your fear and grief. You'll need to keep the discussion going, delving deeper into the details, until you feel some sense of confidence in how you view the tragedy and that you can move past these events. You must find that you're not only safe but also an okay person. How can you be safe or okay if your lover prefers someone else or chooses to inflict pain on you?

Regaining Safety and Control

The most urgent need behind the questions is that of safety and feeling in control of your own destiny. You feel that only full disclosure and information will help you feel safe from being hurt again. You think that if you find out enough information, you'll be able to understand what's happened and perhaps prevent its recurrence. There is certainly truth in that and yet the only person who can truly prevent this from happening again is the offending partner by fully and exclusively committing to you. In her book *Not "Just Friends,"* Shirley Glass explains the importance of coming clean about an affair. Without full disclosure, she argues, the secret remains and holds tremendous sway over the marriage. If your partner has had an affair, he may feel that he's protecting you by not supplying the gritty details. In fact, however, you're already plagued with mental images of the affair, and the real details are needed to replace these horrific fantasies. Only with full disclosure can both of you truly move toward regaining intimacy. This is a terrifying process in which both of you are afraid that you're on the brink of losing your marriage. It is also, however, your chance to grow much closer to each other.

As discussed in Chapter Five, if you don't get answers to your questions, you'll use your imagination to fill in the blanks, based on your history, expectations, and experience. When you first discovered the affair you may have tormented yourself with questions about yourself and whether you are okay.

> How could I have been so stupid?
>
> I *am* stupid; therefore he thinks he can lie to me and it won't matter.
>
> I'm unlovable, so of course she found someone else.
>
> There must be some truth in the names she calls me.
>
> I've put on a few pounds; no wonder he's not interested in me.

Without the recommitment of your partner and honest answers about the affair, you will not be able to adequately answer these questions and move on.

In fact, the rage you feel toward yourself may be more dangerous than your anger at your partner. When people stay angry at a partner over extended periods of time and can't seem to recover, what they're most struggling with is self-doubt. Recovering from the affair then is not only about forgiving the other person but also, more important, understanding and forgiving yourself. This may seem counterintuitive, but inherent in the question "How can I ever trust you again?" resides the more pressing question of "How can I ever trust myself again?" If you can resolve the latter question, the former becomes a little less important.

Information alone will not be sufficient. If you have committed the betrayal, you will also need to offer your partner reassurances that she can feel safe and in control of her world. This may include added accountability for your whereabouts, evidence of your good behavior, or any other means of taking the guesswork out of your relationship—the guesswork that wasn't necessary before the betrayal.

REPTILES IN LOVE

You Ain't Nothin' But a Hound Dog!

James and Beth had been married for eleven years, and both described their relationship as positive and fulfilling. They had three children, enjoyed activities together on a fairly regular basis, and described sex as satisfying . . . until the crisis. Beth discovered that James had been visiting prostitutes. He had also had a brief sexual fling with a neighbor, and, as the family became aware of their problems, one of Beth's sisters revealed that James had made a pass at her as well. The couple entered therapy in tremendous turmoil, with Beth trying to decide whether she could stay with James.

Beth was preoccupied with the details of James's infidelity. She wanted to know where and when he met or approached women. She wanted to know the ages of the women; she wanted to know

(continued on next page)

(continued)

REPTILES IN LOVE
You Ain't Nothin' But a Hound Dog!

about gifts that he had given to strippers and hookers, and she compared these to the gifts he had given her. She felt that she might be able to stay with him if she had enough information to control the possibility of his acting out in the future.

She had almost as many questions for herself as she had for James. Was she attractive enough? Was she tall enough? Did she dress well? Had she said no to sex at some critical time? How could she not have picked up on the clues that something wasn't right? When I asked her to talk about her self-doubts, however, she would stridently claim that she had no such worries and that this was all about James's behavior.

James needed to stop rationalizing his addiction by assuming that it was solely related to his marriage.[1] Obviously, his marriage needed reexamination and constructive change, but his going to prostitutes had become a compulsion for which only he was responsible. It would be the same if James were addicted to drugs, alcohol, spending, or gambling.[2] He needed to decide whether, for him, sexuality had become a dangerous addiction or was a lifestyle choice that he wished to maintain, unfettered by marriage. Clearly he wouldn't be able to stay married if he chose the latter.

Little by little, Beth was able to let down some of her reptilian defenses and talk about how hurt she was and how awful this had made her feel. She attacked less and talked more about doubts she had about herself as a woman. James gradually stopped trying to explain his behavior and showed that he really did recognize the damage he had done. He entered treatment for his sexual addiction in addition to coming to marital counseling. Together James and Beth were able to depersonalize his sexual addiction and view it as his illness, which was not a reflection of some failing on her part. This didn't guarantee that he would never relapse or that Beth would be safe in this relationship. There are no such guarantees. Beth was, however, able to think about herself and her own strengths and needs. She needed to know that she was okay and could survive with or without James. She stopped feeling like damaged goods.

The questions that follow relate to the process of rebuilding. While these are specific to infidelity, you will see that many are related to other betrayals as well. The primary task here is to organize your thinking about your own needs, mental health, and safety, and then to look toward the relationship.

1. Am I convinced that the affair is over?

2. Is my partner holding on to any mementos or other reminders of the affair or in any way hanging on to the person or the experience?

3. Do I trust my partner to work on his part or is he blaming me for his actions?

4. What information do I really need in order to understand it and to feel safer, or more okay, about myself? (Are the questions I'm asking now really helping me?)

5. Do we, as a couple, need some form of ritual together to mark the fact that our relationship has changed? Will this enable us to share the grief?

6. How could my partner convince me that he really understands how badly he has hurt me, that this was unfair, and that I didn't deserve to be treated this way?

7. What kind of apology do I need from my partner?

8. What kinds of protections do I need in order to feel safe in the future?

9. Do I need some form of ritual (funeral) to mark the fact that our relationship has permanently changed and to grieve that loss?

10. What do I fear would happen if I forgave the betrayal too quickly?

11. How would I treat my partner differently if I did begin to forgive the betrayal, and how would I begin the rebuilding of our relationship?

When answering these very specific questions, a couple may find that there are actual behaviors they need to see from their partner in order to feel safe.

In the case of James and Beth, James will most likely have to account for his time much more precisely than he ever had to before. If he must be a half-hour late getting home from work, he'll need to call Beth and explain. He may feel that this is overkill and that he shouldn't have to do this if Beth were really learning to trust him and if everything were going well. Wrong! Even if Beth were to agree that he shouldn't have to account for all of his time, she's only human. She's likely to experience increased anxiety and worry during the unaccounted time—and we already know that anxiety leads to reptilian responses. By the time James does get home, Beth may be well into a reptilian fight-or-flight response that even she doesn't fully understand. Is James's need to feel independent worth this building of tension and fear? Not if they want their relationship to have a chance.

The safer Beth feels, the greater her ability to develop trust in James. It's often helpful for the couple to place time limits on any such checking or other changes in their relationship; for instance, after a period of six months they may wish to review their situation and decide whether checking in regularly is still necessary. It probably will be. In this case, James continued to demonstrate improvement in his own health, a focus on Beth as the center of his life, and an ability to ask Beth for what he needs. Beth similarly improved in her own self-esteem and confidence. Their total focus on one another and their increased intimacy gradually rendered checking and suspiciousness unnecessary.

There's Nothing Going On; We're Just Friends

This kind of betrayal, which often causes the greatest consternation, occurs when there are intense emotional connections between a partner and a friend or coworker, where there appears to be a romantic connection, but there has been no sex.[3] Usually, both partners are aware that the connection with the "friend" is more intense than just a casual friendship. If your partner is in such a relationship, however, he'll probably insist that there's "nothing going on" because he and his friend are not lovers. When you (or your couples therapist) suggest, however, that he place this outside relationship on hold for a while so that you and he can work on your marriage, he may seem shocked and insist that he can't do that. He may defend himself and say that he's not going to allow you to control him and pick his friends.[4]

In such a case, you may be reluctant to confront your partner because you believe him when he says that nothing is going on. At a deeper level, however, you're aware that you don't have his full attention. You may be confused about your own feelings and scold yourself for not being more trusting. He says that nothing is going on, so why should you be so jealous? You probably wonder what's wrong with you, even as you realize that your concerns are not completely groundless.

When evaluating whether you yourself are involved in an emotional infidelity, consider some of the following clues. Would you be comfortable with your partner hearing all discussion between you and your friend? Do you exchange personal information about your intimate partner or your marriage with your friend? Are you focusing on the new relationship more than on your partner? Have you touched your friend in a sexual way? Please see Shirley Glass's book for a more extensive self-evaluation. Some will say that the intense emotional attachment to such a friend is harmless. Although there has not been sexual intercourse, let me emphasize, emotional infidelity is still a dangerous betrayal. Also, you must recognize that in such emotional connections, the next step to sex is usually a very short one and often merely a matter of time and opportunity.

REPTILES IN LOVE

It's Nothing, Really

Cary and Grace came in to see me at Grace's request. She said that they were growing more and more distant from each other, they never did anything fun, and Cary just wasn't interested in her anymore. Cary agreed with all of this—except he insisted that it was Grace who was not interested in him. He described her preoccupation with the children and her house projects and said that she always seemed more interested in her work friends than in him—and especially interested in her colleague Frank.

Cary described Frank as a good guy whom he liked as well. Over the past six months, however, he noticed Grace bringing Frank into all their discussions, meeting him for lunch, and working out with him occasionally at the health club. Cary was intensely aware that Grace talked about joking and laughing with Frank, something he and Grace had not experienced for some time now.

Grace insisted that Cary's jealousy was going to ruin their marriage. She said that Frank was a good friend who was willing to listen to her, which was more than she could expect from Cary. She described the distance in her relationship with Cary as going back a couple of years, since his promotion at work, which seemed to take up all his energy. She was particularly angry that anyone would think for a moment that she would commit adultery. She believed in marriage and would never cheat. Because of these strong beliefs, she felt it was safe and fair for her to have a close male friend.

It's obvious to the most casual reader that Cary and Grace are not in trouble merely because of her "friendship" with Frank. Cary would like to believe that Frank is *the* problem, and Grace would like to believe that Frank is not a problem at all. If they want to move forward, Grace will need to place the relationship with Frank on hold for several months. She must make Cary her priority, exploring and redeveloping her relationship with him. Cary in turn has to trust Grace to do so, and he then must refocus his attention on her. They may need to complete the steps in this book, examining all areas of their relationship and not limiting their stories to his or her job, the kids, his jealousy, or their lack of sex. When they reconnect, fully reengage with one another, a parallel process will occur in which she will be less connected to Frank, and Frank will be less threatening to Cary.

My Partner Hit Me

I have worked with many couples with whom some form of physical violence has occurred. There are many levels of violence but it should be said that no level of physical restraint, hitting, or control can be permissible if a couple is to have a trusting relationship. (I am speaking here of physical aggression without the partner's consent, not of aggression that is part of mutually agreed-on sexual play.) As described in Chapter One, I will not work with a couple when violence has occurred if they cannot commit to a zero tolerance for aggression, or, failing that, separation. This is obviously for safety reasons but also because it is impossible to develop intimacy when one of the partners is fearful. By this point in the book, you understand this as a neurological fact.

When there has been an act of violence, the steps described previously for affairs must also be undertaken. If the violent act was a one-time episode and both partners feel relatively safe, they will still need to go through the process of grieving this incredible breach between them and rebuilding their sense of safety and cooperation. If there have been repeated physical incidents or threats of violence, this will be more complicated and take longer to rebuild. In either case, a therapist will be most often necessary both for negotiating this trauma between the partners and evaluating the contributing factors and safety needs.

My Partner Misused Our Money

For many this may seem like one of the lesser betrayals but financial issues have torn families apart. I have mentioned money problems in Chapter Five and have provided some references in the Resources. It is very important for couples to recognize that money fights are almost never about mere dollars-and-cents; rather, they have to do with power, trust, and independence. Couples who have trouble solving their financial fights are usually stuck because they are not addressing these key relationship issues.

THE MANY FACES OF BETRAYAL: THE LESSER BETRAYALS

It is difficult to divide up betrayals by levels of severity. In reality what constitutes a profound betrayal lies in the eyes of the beholder. The following are some examples of, what I see as, the less crippling acts of betrayal. Obviously, we surprise and confound each other every day in intimate relationships. We accommodate to numerous small and large idiosyncrasies that we had not noticed while dating. Each of these, in their own way, might be seen as a betrayal.

REPTILES IN LOVE
The Case of the Sudden Blonde

Steve surveyed the party with the kind of cool appraising glance that takes in everything and is distracted by nothing. Nothing, that is, until the pulsing, shimmering brightness of a beautiful blonde across the room caught his eye. She glanced at him, and for a moment there was the electric spark of recognition, though they had never met. She smiled at him in a way that would have brought a weaker man to his knees. Trying to remain casual, Steve tossed a look to his wife, Susan. She was glaring at him like a prison yard searchlight. He scanned the room again, purposely avoiding the blonde.

When they returned home after the party, Steve slipped his arms around Susan, pressing his groin against her suggestively. Susan attacked him like Muhammad Ali going after Joe Frazier, and quickly took the first verbal jabs. How could he try to make out with her after lusting after other women all night? Stung and bleeding, Steve threw off a quick dismissal of her claim with the assurance that he never lusted after anyone but her. She clubbed him with a one-word response. He countered with a slashing assessment of their recent sex life, which actually seemed to put her on the ropes a bit, only to bring her back swinging with his lack of caring and cooperation.

At this point Steve decided that this bout was going nowhere fast and countered that they wouldn't have these fights if they had more sex. As soon as he brought up this topic, he recognized that his timing could have been better. Not only was Susan not interested in discussing their sex life, but she hinted that it might be some time before this became an issue again.

To some people, Steve's party flirtation might not seem like a profound betrayal. But to Susan it became a symbol of all her own insecurities and concerns about the status of their relationship. The "story" of her marriage, in which both parties were so in love that they would never even look at anyone else with "lust in their hearts," was shattered. At that point, it didn't matter that the only thing that went on at the party was prolonged eye contact. Steve might as well have slept with the blonde right then and there.

As you can tell from Steve and Susan's story, there are other kinds of betrayal besides having an affair. Lying, for instance, is a betrayal of trust, no matter what the lie is about. If it's a harmless lie ("Do I look fat in these jeans?" "No, dear"), it's not a profound betrayal, and it won't tear the relationship apart. Any betrayal may still have the potential to make the partners less trusting of each other and therefore damage their ability to be intimate.

My Family Comes First

What happens when you're unable to rely on your partner to back you up when friends or family interfere?[5] This can be a catastrophic injury. Take, for instance, Norman and Lizzy. When it was just the two of them, they got along famously and were really good to each other. When they were around Norman's family, however, he would suddenly distance himself from Lizzy. He'd also develop a form of selective deafness that rendered him unable to hear the insulting things his parents said to her.

When Lizzy confronted him about his parents' behavior, he said she "had it in for them" and never wanted to be around them. Norman felt that in order to support Lizzy, he would have to hurt his parents, and he knew that with his family, once you've taken sides, there's no going back. In therapy, he eventually was able to see that he was making the relationship between his parents and Lizzy much more difficult by trying to play both sides. He discovered that he and Lizzy could have nonverbal signals for when she needed his support. In time, he was able to say to his parents, in a calm and non-reptilian way, that insults to Lizzy would no longer be tolerated.

Norman and Lizzy let his family interfere with their respect for each other in an unhealthy way. In such cases, a couple needs to change two things at the same time: they need to reduce these outsiders' influence in safe and structured ways while also increasing their own intimacy. This can be particularly dicey when the outsiders are his and her family members; trying to reconnect as a couple while still respecting the extended families may require several partnership meetings.

Longtime friends can also intrude. You need to surround yourselves with friends who are supportive of your relationship. If you do incorporate a friend or family member into your life who doesn't support your marriage, you and your partner will need to openly discuss the ramifications on your intimacy. You'll need to give exact details about why this person is important to you and how you will defend your relationship against his or her negative influence.

Evolutionary Tip
Beware the Controlling Partner

Choosing to make friends or family a greater priority than one's partner is often related to difficulties with intimacy. This may not be the case, however, if a controlling partner is trying to make you abandon your family. This is a dangerous situation. It has been noted in cases of spousal abuse that the perpetrator often attempts to separate the victim from family and friends in order to better control her. It's absolutely critical that you maintain your freedom and autonomy and healthy relationships with friends and family as you increase your intimacy with your partner.

My Needs Have Changed

Another form of betrayal occurs when one of the partners discovers or admits to some new need or priority that has never before been addressed between them. This may be a somewhat negotiable need, such as discovering that you love education and want to return to school or that you want to quit your job to be a full-time rodeo clown. But perhaps you and your partner had decided not to have children, and one day your partner says, "I suddenly realize that I really want a child." Is this premeditated betrayal? In most cases, it is not, but nevertheless it's a betrayal in that it's a breach of the original contract you made with each other. Therefore, it may well bring up the same kinds of reptilian feelings—anger, grief, and mistrust—as any other betrayal.

In some cases, the new situation is not negotiable. I've worked with a number of couples, for instance, in which one of the partners has discovered or finally admitted that he or she is homosexual. For religious or family reasons, a partner may never have admitted, even to himself, that he was most attracted to other men. You and your partner may have a wonderful friendship in every other aspect of your lives together, but the humiliation and the question of what this means to you as someone who thought she was in a heterosexual relationship can be devastating. There may also be a bit of relief that some of the distance you felt in your relationship finally makes sense. You and your partner are now faced with all kinds of questions. Can you maintain any kind of friendship? If so, what form will it take? Just like any other partner who is suddenly left for another person, you may feel overwhelmed by this sudden loss.

Our Roles Have Changed

Partners usually take on certain roles in their relationship; in Chapter Three we talked about the stories we develop about each other. One partner may be the breadwinner, one may be the caretaker; one may be the disciplinarian, the other the peacemaker. What happens when the breadwinner decides he wants to be the stay-at-home dad? What happens when the shy wallflower decides she has to see what's out there in the world? The partner can perceive this kind of change as a huge betrayal. Even if your partner loses weight or quits alcohol or drug abuse, such a change in identity and everyday habit can create a sea change and even a feeling of betrayal of the previous relationship agreement.

Such changes can also represent a degree of danger. I've seen numerous couples in which a relationship crisis was precipitated by a change that one would expect to be positive. If your partner suddenly loses weight and looks more sexually appealing, will she find other opportunities? Will she still be interested only in you? Many couples in which one or both are alcoholic become estranged after the drinking stops.[6] If your partner begins to change in her self-confidence, interests, style of relating, means of defending herself, or even her schedule, it's normal for you to feel somewhat threatened. Such changes require you to change too. Although you might be tempted to cling to the safety of your old ways, ideally you'll be able to turn this "danger" into an opportunity to revive your curiosity about your mate and learn to blend the best of the old with the new. If your partner is wanting to be more active, you might spend one evening exploring her new interests or trying out something new for the two of you and then spend another evening cuddled on the sofa watching television like a couple of old "couch potatoes."

THE SEARCH FOR CLOSURE

The amount of damage caused by the betrayal can be measured by how the betrayed partner feels. If you have been sufficiently traumatized, you'll need to do more than just resolve the immediate issue. You'll need to rebuild your faith and trust in yourself, in your partner, in others, and perhaps in the world. What do you do when you realize that many of your truths about your lover, your relationship, and yourself are suddenly in doubt? How do you get past the terrible mistrust of your lover, the damage to your hopes for the future? How do you learn to trust yourself again? Much of this chapter details steps toward what therapists describe as *closure*.

Closure is an elusive term; it embodies aspects of forgiveness,[7] understanding, reassurance, security, and self-exploration, among others. To regain emotional health, one must be able to move beyond past events. Reaching closure means that you are sufficiently comfortable with the information and commitments you have been given, so that for you the incident feels "closed." This does not mean the betrayal is forgotten but that you are able to move on to new business, such as resolving other problems and developing your intimacy.

Obviously, that's not easy to do when past events include an affair. With such massive turmoil in your world, the Reptilian Brain springs into action. Along with all the deficits of memory and thinking we've talked about, there are also the urges to run away or do harm. To move beyond the "betrayal experience," you will need to reexamine your needs, your beliefs about yourself, and what you can expect from your partner as realistically and as dispassionately as possible.

As discussed, closure in the most dramatic betrayals, such as infidelity, will require extensive discussions of details and slow rebuilding of the relationship. In a lesser betrayal, such as a partner's wanting to take night classes when the other expects him or her to be home at night, achieving closure may be somewhat less complicated. The "betrayer" in this case may need to reassure the partner that this decision is not about being unhappy in the marriage. The other may also need to know that even with less time together, the two of them will still find ways to enhance their intimacy. Knowing why the partner is seeking higher education may resolve whether there is any threat connected to it.

Responsibility and Guilt

Relationship issues are not resolved by determining that your partner is sick—as tempting as that might be. It is critical to eliminate the overpowering feeling of responsibility you may sometimes feel for your partner's mood, health, attitude, and behavior. This allows you to make clearer decisions as to whether your partner is good for you—as opposed to asking the self-destructive question, "Why am I not good enough to be treated better?"

This doesn't mean that you're absolved from all responsibility when your partner acts out. If you've been in numerous unhealthy relationships, for example, a more important question than whether you deserve to be treated well is, "What attracts me to people who don't treat me well?"

Thinking "My husband drinks and hits me because I'm not good in bed" can lead only to disaster. Thinking "My wife cheated on me because I don't make enough money and have erectile dysfunction" won't contribute to your ability to forgive her, nor will it lead to realistic relationship decisions. Such a thought serves only to increase defeat and rage.

In contrast, an accurate accounting for responsibility in a relationship can be extremely helpful. "My wife became attached to another man while I was ignoring her and the kids and spending all my energy at work" might be a rational and treatable issue. Instead of labeling yourself as incompetent, unlovable, underendowed, or bad in bed, you are focusing on a temporary, reparable behavior.

You may feel overwhelming guilt for what you have done, if you committed the betrayal, or for any possible contribution to the betrayal on your part, if you are the victim. Such guilt may be related to the current relationship but also driven by old stories from childhood. Many of us carry messages from our past that we are unlovable, that we should not expect to be treated well, or that if someone harms us, then it must be our fault. We feel guilty or defeated when bad things happen, even if we really had no part in causing them. You will only be able to deal with these feelings of guilt effectively if you calm and protect yourself and begin to analyze your actions. If you have committed some wrong or allowed yourself to be harmed, you will want to look at how you will recover and prevent this from happening again. Remaining in a position of guilt and self-recrimination prevents you from moving on and rebuilding. Such despair may, in fact, set up either partner for further negative behavior.

Closure and Grief

A favorite poem of mine is W. H. Auden's depiction of perfect despair, *Funeral Blues*. In this devastating description of grief, there is terrible loss, but at least there is ritual. On the day of the funeral, time is stopped, noises are silenced, and black-and-white decorations declare that life is never going to be the same. There is, however, one line in the poem that describes betrayal as much as it describes death: "I thought that love would last for ever: I was wrong."

I've often heard it said, sometimes a little sheepishly, that it's easier to grieve a death than a divorce or betrayal. In death, the partner didn't usually leave voluntarily or choose someone else. In what way might a couple acknowledge that because of some thoughtless act, they'll never feel quite the same way about each other again? How, except with screaming, tears, and accusations, do they express the feeling that, in Auden's words, "nothing now can ever come to any good"?[8]

It's the inability to understand and express the unbelievable and inexpressible that prevents us from taking the next step. We get stuck in confusion and hopelessness because we can't get answers and don't feel heard in our pain. This is frequently the sticking point in moving through grief and closure. As the offending partner is repeatedly questioned and challenged, and resists giving answers, he finds it impossible to really feel close to his partner, which in turn raises her anxiety level. The cycle continues. She gets no relief if the questioning doesn't result in satisfying answers, and he questions whether anything can ever repair the damage. She interprets his despair as a lack of remorse and wonders if he is really sorry or even sure about staying. In order to step out of this cycle, she may find some way of alerting her partner to more of what she needs and that there is really to be an end to the questions. If he can step out of the cycle by finding a new way to offer information or reassurance then they will be able to move on.

A part of this rebuilding will be learning to grieve together, even though everyone's grief is experienced and handled in different ways. Remember that initially the two partners are grieving different aspects of the relationship and the betrayal, potentially with one grieving for the loss of the affair partner. As the couple becomes less adversarial and more trusting of one another, they will need to acknowledge together, that their relationship will never be the same. The injured partner may never trust the other as blindly as she had before. There may have been other losses along the way as well, such as legal problems (in the case of domestic violence), loss of mutual friendships (in the case of an affair), or other injuries. The couple may need a formal ritual together, like a funeral of sorts or at bare minimum an intimate discussion of these losses and how they hope to continue on. Their relationship will never be the same but with a good deal of work, it may be better.

The most important message I have for you is that *all* major changes in life represent a crisis for the relationship at some level. If the crisis is related to an internal threat, such as an affair, there's going to be greater perceived danger, but even threats from the outside require adjustments in the relationship. At their worst, couples remain stuck in their grief and rage, learn nothing, and ruin a large piece of their lives. At their best, couples incorporate the shock and new learning about each other into their relationship, grieve the losses they incur, and begin to rebuild their own spirits as well as their relationship. They reawaken their curiosity about each other and enliven their intimacy.

The complexities of dealing with strong emotions, self-examination, self-protection, and attempts to reach an understanding with your partner can be overwhelming. I hope that if you experience such injuries, you'll seek out supportive people to talk to and any other help available. That's why I've included the next chapter, an introduction to couples therapy. It will describe couples therapy, give you tips on how to find a therapist, and explain what you can expect to accomplish for yourself and your relationship.

9

Reptiles in Therapy
An Introduction to Couples Therapy

Jenkins's therapist beamed at him and announced,
"That's it. You're completely cured of your delusions.
Congratulations."
*   "But what about all these butterflies on me?"*
Jenkins cried, jumping up and brushing at himself
frantically.
*   "Well for heaven's sake, man," yelled the shrink,*
"don't get them on me!"

As you've read through this book, you've been introduced to a number of couples in the Reptiles in Love boxes. These are composites of case studies from my therapeutic practice, although obviously no person is described specifically. I hope you've come away from these case studies with three ideas:

1. You are not alone. It's hard to be humans in love, especially when our primitive reptilian instincts fight so fiercely to be heard.

2. The reptile doesn't always win. Evolution can and does take place when partners are willing to look at themselves and their relationships from an objective, caring perspective.

3. Sometimes it takes an outsider, such as a couples therapist, to help people really understand how they can get beyond seemingly impassible barriers.

The focus of this chapter is on point 3. Now that you've become somewhat familiar with the idea of couples therapy, I'm going to let you see just how the process works. I'm going to review a typical couples treatment, as I practice it, from start to finish.

When a couple decides to undergo relationship counseling, they're usually scared. They may not want to admit it, and they handle this anxiety in any number of ways, but they're frightened. It is, after all, an unusual event to go into a stranger's office and describe your most intimate problems. The purpose of this chapter is to help make the process a bit easier on you, should you decide to give it a try.

CHOOSING A MARITAL THERAPIST

As is true of any other professional offering, finding a therapist for you and your partner can be confusing. It's a huge step, and choosing the wrong therapist may harm your relationship more than it helps. The "rules" for interpersonal relationships are not very well defined, and what works well for one couple may not suit another. There are many approaches to couples therapy and many good and skilled therapists. To begin your search, there are two very important steps you should take:

1. Get recommendations from people you trust.
2. Check credentials.

Getting Recommendations

You may know a couple who has already seen a therapist and thought well of him or her. Don't ask your friends for specifics of what went on in therapy, but do ask them what they thought of the therapist's demeanor, knowledge, and professionalism. Be aware, however, that if you do see a therapist who has already seen a friend or family member, she won't share information with you about that friend or family member and in fact won't even acknowledge having seen the person unless she has permission to do so.

In addition to speaking with friends, consider other resources for recommendations. I hope you feel comfortable discussing your family with your physician. Your doctor may know a therapist to whom he or she regularly refers people or have other excellent resources available.

Speaking of your family physician, relationship problems are often caused or exacerbated by medical issues. If you're irritable due to lack of sleep, blood pressure issues, sugar digestion problems, thyroid disorders, or any other medical problems, even the most brilliant psychotherapy won't alleviate these disorders or their impact on your relationship. It's always a good idea to rule out medical contributions to the problem first. This can be enormously relieving and also point the way to further interventions.

Other professionals in your life may be good sources of recommendations. Your religious adviser may offer counseling within his or her training or refer you to reputable persons whom he or she trusts. Attorneys who regularly work with divorce or mediation may also know reputable clinicians in the area.

Checking Credentials

There are many different kinds of therapists, and it's easy to get confused by their various titles. A psychiatrist holds an M.D. degree, which means he or she trained as a physician and is licensed to prescribe medications in addition to psychotherapy. A psychologist holds either a doctorate of philosophy (Ph.D.) or a psychology doctorate (Psy.D.), but is not a medical doctor (and is therefore unable to prescribe medication, at this time. There is a movement to allow specially trained psychologists prescription privileges.). A psychologist can offer psychological testing as part of the evaluation process.

A master's-prepared clinician is a person who holds a master's degree in social work, psychology, or other related field. The clinician with a master's degree would have such initials as M.S.W. (master of social work), M.A. or M.S. (master of arts or master of sciences), or L.C.S.W. (licensed clinical social worker). The licensure title may vary between states. Any of the professionals listed here can perform couples therapy, provided that they have had additional training or supervision (or both) in marriage and family therapy.

When you're choosing a marital therapist, the educational degree should not be the deciding factor. Research has shown that success in treatment depends greatly on the relationship between you and your therapist, and that the experience, personality, and compatibility of your therapist are all important factors.[1] This is not to disparage the therapist's level of training as unimportant; you do want a therapist with appropriate training and preparation, as well as someone with a good reputation, considering that anyone can call himself or herself a counselor. But having the right credentials doesn't mean that the therapist is right for you. It does at least narrow the field and assures you that this person has accomplished the basic training and skill development requirements and has been supervised in clinical practice.

I do suggest that you seek a therapist who is licensed to practice in your state. Certain titles are protected—thus in most states the title of psychologist or psychotherapist, for example, can be used only by persons with the required training. In addition to minimum training and supervision requirements (in most states two years of supervision is required for licensure), licensure generally requires continuing education, which gives you some assurance that a licensed therapist is keeping up with the field. Licensure also means that you can check on whether there are formal complaints filed against the therapist and that you have recourse with the state licensing agency if the therapist fails to provide services within the requirements and ethics of the profession.

You can contact the American Association of Marriage and Family Therapists, the National Register for Health Service Providers, the American Psychiatric Association, the national or state divisions of the American Psychological Association, the National Association of Social Workers, or your state's Medical Society chapter for lists of providers in your area. Please see the list of these organizations at the end of the Resources. Professional societies have requirements for membership and continuing education and also provide oversight and the possibility of disciplinary action against an errant professional.

There are, of course, many other considerations that may affect your decision to seek help and with whom to work. Your health insurance, the experience of your initial interview with the therapist, and your sense of whether the therapist is hearing you will all be important factors in your decision.

Health Insurance

If you anticipate using your health benefits for couples counseling, there are a few matters of which you should be aware. First, most health insurance programs don't cover couples therapy. However, if there's a diagnosable mental or medical condition requiring treatment through a family approach, many insurers will cover therapy, and some even encourage family or marital interventions. If you're in a managed care or preferred provider health insurance system, that program will have a list of approved providers.

The good news is that these providers have already met basic licensure and state requirements in order to be approved for the list. Some insurers are better than others at actually encouraging additional training and exceptional care from its providers. The bad news is that your choices may be limited. It could be that the person your neighbor raved about is not on your insurer's provider list.

You must then decide whether to try one of the covered providers or to pay out of pocket to see your neighbor's recommended therapist. You can petition your insurer to cover the provider you want, but most managed care companies want to see very strong evidence that this person provides some form of treatment not available through their contracted providers.

First Encounters

Because couples are all different, there is no perfect couples therapist who can work well with everyone. Couples seeking help for their relationship must be careful to choose someone with whom they both feel safe. If, as the process of therapy begins, either of you is feeling judged or attacked by the therapist, challenge him or consider asking for a referral to someone else. It's unlikely that your marriage will benefit from continued work with that person, unless you specifically handle your concern. If the therapist is seen as overly agreeing with one of the partners, he has joined the problem. Therapy is over unless the three of you handle this issue directly. Because both partners' Reptilian Brains are aroused and expecting attack, they may at any moment feel as though the therapist is "taking sides," but with a skilled therapist this will balance out.

The therapist must, however, evaluate each individual diagnostically. If a therapist were to continue treating the couple's issues while ignoring clear indications of depression, for example, in one of the partners, there will likely be a negative outcome. Work on the relationship might improve the individual's depressive symptoms, but it's also possible that the depressive symptoms will worsen or intrude in the relationship work (or both).

A determination that one of the partners has symptoms of a mental health issue doesn't suggest that he or she is primarily responsible for the relationship problems. These symptoms would simply be incorporated into the focus on the relationship, the same as any of the other myriad issues that each individual brings to the table. The diagnosed partner may need to be referred for further help, such as individual therapy or an evaluation for medication. The marital therapy will continue to concentrate on the relationship. It is extremely important that neither the couple nor the therapist see the couples work as focusing on one partner's symptoms. In most cases this will lead to the end of the marital work. Both partners need to feel that they are being heard in their entirety and not just as a diagnosis or problem.

Being Heard

For couples counseling to offer hope, the therapist must hear and understand your issues and concerns. If you believe that the therapist thinks your problems are foolish, or if you in any other way feel diminished by the therapist, you'll feel shut out of the process. You would be ill advised to remain in therapy with this person. It's hard enough to defend yourself against your spouse, let alone feel ganged up on by two people: this would push you further into your reptilian state. You might dislike or mistrust the therapist because of something he or she actually did wrong, or because of an instinctual feeling. If there has been an error on the therapist's part, you can often work it out. If you have a deeply felt, instinctual misgiving, then perhaps it's better to move on.

To remedy a perceived error or misstep by the therapist, you need to state your concerns. When a *competent* therapist hears that he has been perceived as one-sided or flippant or dismissive, he will not only correct this but closely examine his own motivations or behaviors. This can be incredibly helpful to the success of the therapy in general. If this wound, however, has been too major for one of you, or if one of you feels that it would simply take too long and too much effort to win back trust, then by all means, seek a different therapist. That is your right.

―――――――

Having said all this, I want to remind you that the therapist's role is only a small part of the changes in your relationship. The real work of the marriage is accomplished between you and your partner in your daily lives, not in the therapist's office. The few hours you spend with me or any other therapist are merely a catalyst. If you learn nothing else in therapy, my hope is that you'll learn that it can be safe to listen to each other and that there are ways for you to recommit to each other. Then the work of developing intimacy will really take off.

THE PROCESS OF THERAPY

Every couple is different, and the course of every therapy is unique. Nevertheless there are specific points along the way that are similar, including the following discrete steps that summarize how I, for one, like to work.

The Initial Evaluation Session

The purpose of the intake or evaluation meeting is mainly to gather information. Therapists will approach this session in different ways, but many will ask you to come early for your first session in order to fill out forms before meeting. These forms will ask about basic demographics including your name, address, and educational background, as well as some family, health, and social history. It's to your advantage to fill out these forms fully; doing so gives the therapist a lot of information in a quick and organized manner. I have certainly had patients refuse to fill out the forms or only fill them out partially, but that just means that I'm going to take more time asking those same questions and making notes.

In our initial discussion, I ask for additional information about the couple's relationship history, their individual mental and physical health histories, family backgrounds, work history, and their reasons for coming in. I then offer a brief overview of my approach, with a quick description of Reptilian Brain functioning.

Often during the intake session, I describe the typical concerns that partners have about coming in for therapy, and let the couple know that these are useful considerations and not impediments. I note that in my view, couples therapy should not be about gluing the relationship back together at all costs. Rather, it should invite the couple to more accurately, objectively, and creatively view each other and the contract between them and look for areas of repair. This is a tall order and may not immediately sound very satisfying. It is my belief, however, that if the couple can accomplish this task, it's likely they won't need to leave each other.

Evolutionary Tip
Ask Questions

During the intake session, you and your partner should ask questions too. You should ask if the therapist has had specific training in couples therapy and if he or she has worked with a large number of couples or families. (If the therapist is new to working with couples but is being formally supervised, he or she can still offer very good treatment. We all have to start somewhere.) Other questions may be specific to your situation. For example, a gay couple will want to know if the therapist is comfortable with and respectful of issues related to homosexuality. A Christian couple may not need to see a "Christian counselor," but they do need to know that the therapist will be respectful of their beliefs.

Establishing Initial Goals

The initial goal of treatment is not increased intimacy, but you already know that. In fact, the initial goal of therapy is to draw back a bit and lessen the intensity, out of respect for the reptilian response to stress, threat, and insult described in the first chapter. When you go through therapy, you need to be more creative, thoughtful, empathic, and organized, not more stimulated and overwhelmed. You don't need to feel pushed into greater intimacy.

When couples first hear that the initial goal of treatment is not intimacy, they generally have mixed reactions. By the time they come to see me, they haven't been doing very well together for some time. The chances that they're going to dance out of my office after the first couple of sessions with newfound respect and thoughts of romance are highly unlikely. Again, it's just too much pressure.

And although the partners may well feel some relief at not being pressured to "get intimate," they may also feel apprehension. At least one of them may be thinking "My god, it sounds like it'll be six months before we ever have sex again." In reality, once they slow down and drop their defenses, most couples are soon able to think more clearly about closeness, intimacy, and sex.

After the Initial Session

Following the initial session, I don't generally ask couples to make a follow-up appointment. Instead, I ask them to go home and briefly discuss the intake, my approach to treatment, and whether I'm the right therapist for them. It may be one or two weeks until I can see the couple again, and I ask them *not* to work on the relationship in the interim. This is very important but, of course, very difficult. You may think that now that you're seeing a shrink, you should go home and be good clients and work on your relationship. I believe that you should take a break from doing this. The urgent need to fix each other will usually result in your engaging in more of the behaviors that have already proved unhelpful. Why add to the sense of hopelessness? In some particularly tense situations, I even encourage a type of in-home separation; I ask couples to be formal and polite with each other, but not to engage in any real discussion of their relationship.

Experiments in Change

Within the first sessions, I remind the partners of something I've said several times in this book: that because no one can tell any two people how to be successful as a couple, every attempted change can be only a working experiment. This is important, because the partners themselves may make errors in what they ask for. The therapist is not omniscient and won't know exactly what behaviors will be most helpful. By the same token, partners may wish for some behavior or favor from the other and then realize that it wasn't exactly what they wanted after all. This doesn't mean that the partners are jerking each other around; it means that they're both exploring options.

You and your partner need permission to ask for things from each other and then alter these requests as you learn more about yourself and each other. If you or your partner views a change in a request as just another rejection ("Nothing I do is good enough for you"), it can be quite devastating and lead to still more mistrust. If you do end up feeling jerked around or manipulated by your partner's requests, then that mistrust is the more immediate problem. A skilled therapist will help you reexamine these problematic requests and research what has caused you to become stuck.

The First Therapeutic Discussion

As noted earlier, after the first session I recommend that you and your partner have a twenty- to thirty-minute discussion focusing only on (1) whether you want to continue with therapy and (2) whether the therapist you chose is the right person for you to see. These are critical decision points. Both partners should be interested in pursuing help, and both partners must feel confidence and safety with the therapist. In this discussion, try to stay businesslike and on the subject. This is not a discussion about what either of you has said in the intake session, nor is it a review of your complaints about each other. It is merely discussion of a specific question: Do you want to continue therapy with this therapist? If for any reason you don't feel that there is a good fit, or if you feel uncomfortable with the therapist, say so, and ask him if he can refer you to a colleague who might be a better match.

The Individual Focus

Once the couple has committed to continuing therapy with me, I ask the partners to focus on themselves individually during the time between the first and second sessions. Remember, all couples work is also individual therapy. The partners are repeatedly encouraged to focus on their own parts in the relationship, encompassing their daily behavior with their partner, their physical and mental health, their family history, their strengths and weaknesses, and their values, among other things. These considerations also include their individual fantasies of who they want to be and what would constitute a good relationship. It's a terrific challenge for partners to pull away from the more comfortable focus on each other's problems and misdeeds and to look at their own contributions to the relationship troubles. Once they're able to do this, a miracle happens: they begin to be less blaming and fault-finding, and we can begin to work on their relationship. You, having read this book, are now way ahead of the game, given the assessments you have already completed.

The Relationship Focus

As much as I have insisted that the partners focus on themselves and their individual needs and contributions, *my* focus is on the contract between them. I'm not interested in who did what first or who did the worst thing, but in the intimate mechanics of their interactions. This focus avoids the one-sided view that both partners may hold: "If my partner would only [insert your belief about your partner here], then we would have a good relationship." I look at family histories and traditions and the stories that have developed between the partners (concepts with which you are well acquainted by now). I particularly look for minimal interventions that provide some hope that things can be better. These are important because all real change happens at deep levels, with small positive acts, even though couples tend to hope for more dramatic changes. Many couples have reported tearful, joyous reconciliations replete with vows and commitments, only to feel defeated and betrayed when they can't keep their promises. It's actually natural and predictable that these dramatic moments don't hold. The moving, heartfelt, violins-in-the-background moments of recommitment don't last. They don't resolve what caused the difficulties in the first place.

I'm really sorry to rain on your parade if you had hoped that your treatment would lead to a magical movie moment. Virtually every area of science incorporates the concept that environments and organisms will gravitate back to their steady state or most familiar level of functioning, and therapy is no exception (see the discussion of relapse in Chapter Six). As you make changes in your intimate relationship, you will be sorely tempted to return to old behaviors, particularly when you're tired, anxious, angry, frightened, or stressed out. The temptation to use your most familiar defenses, such as being sarcastic, yelling, running away, or shutting down, will emerge, and you will make mistakes. These are not signs that you're failing to work on your relationship; they're signs that you are normal human beings.

The Accordion Effect

In fact, the greater the changes we make, the more we are pulled back to the familiar. You and your partner are subconsciously wise enough to know that three or four sessions with a therapist won't resolve your deeper issues. Yet when things start to improve and you're in your initial "honeymoon" period in treatment, you may be struck by the fear that this won't last. Then, as I described in Chapter Six, you have a dramatic and devastating fight. At its worst, this fight makes you both feel that all change was illusory and that there's really no hope for your relationship. At its best, it reminds you that there's still much to do and opens up a new level of commitment. I view this moment as the true beginning of therapy.

A friend once explained that right after she became engaged, she began to act "like a bitch." She hypothesized that subconsciously she wanted her future husband to see her negative side and wanted to know whether he would stick with her through good and bad.

Another possible interpretation relates to the "accordion effect." This is the tendency for people to draw very near to each other and experience intense intimacy—which promptly overwhelms them. In response to feeling overwhelmed, one partner will avoid the other or push him away. This can be a pronounced pattern in some couples, and it is seen, to varying degrees, in all kinds of human interactions. It has also been described, for example, in the study of international conflicts. When two nations in conflict move too quickly toward agreement, they often will suddenly and dramatically reemphasize their differences.

In relationship therapy, partners often surprise themselves with warm feelings toward each other. When this occurs too early, you may feel as though you're giving in too easily. You may feel that you're letting your partner off the hook and that this will be a setup for you to be hurt again. You and your partner will then commit another act of warfare in order to reassert your independence and self-protection. These accordion effects will reduce rapidly as you and your partner learn to trust each other again.

Relapse, or the accordion effect, is actually a healthy indicator that there is more work to be done. It can serve to remind you of these concepts:

1. It's always possible to revert to a reptilian response under the right conditions. Remember that what you're learning here, you're learning in your neocortex (new brain). When you feel threatened, this new information becomes inaccessible, one hopes for only a brief time.[2]
2. You need not take responsibility for your partner.
3. You and your partner truly care about each other and are not out to do harm.
4. Your anger at each other is a learning moment and a sign that slippage has occurred.

5. You need something from each other and are blocked from asking for it.

6. You have an opportunity here to grow together, but you must first stop the damage.

7. You need to stop, breathe, center yourself, and ask, "What is really important to me right now?"

How Long Does Therapy Last?

Therapy proceeds at the pace the couple can tolerate. I don't usually see couples for long periods of time, but I will see them for however long they require. I see couples for an average of ten sessions over a period of approximately four months. A relationship, however, should be an ever developing, organic arrangement, in which the couple continues to grow both individually and in their intimacy. Therefore, I've seen couples over longer time periods, and I've seen couples as returning clients after a hiatus of a year or more. Such returns are generally focused on additional areas of personal growth or on a new external development. The point is that all couples are different, and once they settle down and become open to the process, they bring their own particular mastery and creativity to their problems. Not long after therapy begins, the partners begin to teach me about their marriage and how they intend to fix things. I've seen incredible creativity in the art of adoring a person, once the partners get past their reptilian defenses.

There is one more chapter that needs to be included in this book, and that's a chapter on divorce. Not every story has a happy ending. For some couples, divorce may be the best solution. Chapter Ten focuses on how and why to make this decision and how to see it through in the least reptilian manner possible.

10

Pure Divorce

If You Must, End and Leave Fully Human

Ae fond kiss, and then we sever!
Ae fareweel, and then forever!
But to see her was to love her,
Love but her, and love for ever.
Had we never lov'd sae kindly,
Had we never lov'd sae blindly,
Never met—or never parted—
We had ne'er been broken-hearted.
　　　　　Robert Burns, "Ae Fond Kiss" (1791)

Does it seem at all odd to include a chapter on divorce in a book about saving relationships? (By the way, when I speak about divorce, I mean any kind of breakup, in any kind of intimate relationship.) It may, but as a couples therapist, I would be remiss to leave it out. People come to me because their relationships are in trouble; they're often at their wit's end and are feeling helpless and hopeless. They feel that they're stuck and miserable and out of options.

People do better when they have options, when they don't feel themselves backed into a corner. Divorce is one possible response to marital tension, at the bottom of the list for sure, but to rule it out entirely can make couples feel even more hopeless. They may actually feel more desperate, frantic, primitive, and reptilian—because they have no choices and feel as though they're up against a wall. Ultimately they will be better served if they can freely decide to stay together and work on redeveloping their relationship on the basis of their wants and needs, rather than staying because there is no other possibility. So in this chapter, we'll explore divorce from the reptilian perspective and how, if it is the option you ultimately choose, you can separate in a humane, and human, way.

It would be great if everyone were very careful and smart in their choice of partners and then tried, in every way, to be faithful to that decision. Sometimes, however, even when people truly think they have been careful and have tried everything, they still end up choosing to leave. In this book, we've explored methods for preserving and increasing intimacy. Now it's only natural that we examine the decision to leave a relationship and the attempt to move on to a healthy life.

Divorce may be the single most devastating event a person will ever experience. The pain and tension that occur, leading up to and throughout the rituals and legalities of divorce, can damage a person's self-esteem, faith in the world, and sense of safety. If your partner says you're no longer the right person, you may begin to doubt yourself. You may question your intelligence, competence, and attractiveness. I remember a psychologist friend of mine who was strongly opposed to medication for most mental health issues. During the proceedings of his own divorce, however, he suggested that perhaps everyone going through the process should be heavily medicated until it runs its course. Many people have expressed, somewhat ashamedly, the feeling that it would have been easier to accept the death of their partner than the devastation of divorce. As we saw in Chapter Eight, at least with death there's a funeral, a formal ritual for closure and grief.

You've probably been amazed and horrified by stories of people who seem willing to go to any length, including self-destructive behavior or harm to their children, in order to continue their battle with their former partners. I've seen couples readily blow through their children's college funds in attorney fees, "for the principle of the thing." Such rage and recklessness seem incomprehensible to most outsiders, particularly if they haven't been through divorce themselves. The need to defend the self and to combat the partner's unjust and evil behavior can be overpowering—and represents the worst, most destructive kind of primitive reptilian behavior.

PURE DIVORCE

Pure may seem like an odd adjective to attach to something as difficult and profound as divorce. I use it to imply the clear decision by two people not to be a couple any longer and therefore to abandon all rights and responsibilities regarding each other. *Pure* suggests the clean separation from all the messy entanglements of caretaking, influence, betrayals, and so on of an intimate relationship. I encourage couples to strive for pure divorce[1] but also recognize what a lofty goal this can be. I think it's the most highly evolved and least painful method of separation. Pure divorce requires that you remove yourself emotionally from the old relationship; focus on your own needs, fears, and personality; and release all claims on the other person. This goes back to something I've repeated throughout this book: all couples work is individual work. For pure divorce to occur, you must be willing to stop focusing on your partner and focus only on yourself. When people are able to examine themselves, they attend to their own needs instead of guessing and fretting about their former partner's needs or crimes. We're often more willing to focus on others, to an obsessive degree, than to examine ourselves. Group therapy participants often remark that they can easily see the errors that other participants are making in their lives, long before they recognize the same errors in themselves. The desire to continue to battle with your former partner helps you avoid self-examination. It's an addictive need in the sense that all addictions are partially related to an avoidance of one's self. This addiction is to the dead relationship and, like any addiction, is an unhealthy attachment that keeps you from focusing on personal issues that you need to address.

Combative relationships can go on long after the divorce and even beyond the development of new relationships. It's truly sad to see a person who is supposedly in a brand new relationship but refuses to leave the old one. In spite of her new love and supposed new life, she retains such rage at her previous partner that she in fact remains in the old, dead relationship. Such a person can never fully engage in the new relationship as long as she holds on to the old one.

When divorcing, partners are often unwilling to truly move on and let go of all influential connections to the other. They feel confused about why the relationship went wrong. The most satisfying answer to the raging doubts about themselves is that their partner's behavior was the problem. They may even feel as though they're giving pertinent and helpful advice that will help their partner in his or her future life. Such comments as "You really need to watch your drinking and driving," "In your next relationship, maybe you should try not to lie and cheat," or the inspiring "Maybe with your new girlfriend you should try to be less of a jackass" may seem to be reasonable and caring recommendations.

Once you've opted for divorce, you've generally lost credibility with each other. That doesn't mean that you're wrong. It simply means that your partner can no longer *hear* you. You're both protecting yourselves and rightfully so . . . for the present. (This condition may change even in a contentious divorce, when both persons properly grieve and move on.) You can't take in any real or perceived criticism without the danger of further injury. In this state, you may hear the simple, helpful phrase "You should wear your coat today; it's really cold" as "You're really far too stupid to dress yourself properly."

In pure divorce, you try, with all your might, to truly say goodbye to your former relationship and not act on instincts for revenge, justice, or even helpfulness. You will succeed at this only when you've reached a conclusion that you indeed are giving up on rec-onciliation, at least for the present.

You'll be able to get on with your life only if you can truly let go of the guilt, recriminations, and urge for vengeance surrounding your loss. This is the essence of grief.

Avoiding the Reptilian Brain's Influence on Divorce

Any major life transition creates some level of threat. The most alarming crisis will be one that threatens your strongly held beliefs or sense of safety, and ending an intimate relationship certainly meets this criterion; it's only natural that reptilian defenses will be activated. Pain, fear, and tension lead to primitive responses. The reptilian defense, you will remember, allows only for attack or escape. There is no middle ground when the Reptilian Brain dominates. We excuse our rage-filled, embarrassing actions as being justified by our partner's unholy evil. Our sense of defeat and hopelessness demands an answer.

Without reasonable answers, however, the injured person may resort to petty acts of terrorism, which can be neither forgotten nor forgiven. They may include behaviors that end up harming not just the "guilty" partner but other loved ones as well, particularly chil-dren. For example, it's not uncommon for an injured spouse to inform the children that "Daddy is out with his whore" or that "Mommy loves her new boyfriend more than she loves you." One can only hope that these parents will eventually regret inflicting these injuries on their children. Unfortunately, by then the damage has already been done.

Not all relationships end with rage, but many do. It seems that once the betrayals mount to the degree that the relationship is dying, self-preservation of the most primitive variety becomes most important. We lash out in order to protect ourselves and prove that the partner was the problem. If we later feel guilt for negative be-havior during the divorce, we're likely to claim temporary insanity or that we acted under extreme duress, but does that really help?

Reptilian Decisions Lead to Bad Divorces

Divorce is a last resort, but, in the case of two people who are committed to this course, it might just be the best solution. Rather than saying that they failed at marriage, we can say that they finally wised up and discovered that life was too short to spend it torturing each other. On the one hand, there's no doubt that some folks are too quick to threaten or pursue divorce when they haven't extended enough effort to examine their relationship. On the other hand, it may be that the desperation many of us feel for saving marriages actually makes the situation worse instead of better. What may be most important is that both partners clearly examine why they are prepared to end the relationship and what they hope to gain from this step.

Often divorces involve at least one person believing that she'll be a better person if she's with a better person. Perhaps these people have found that when they feel like a jerk themselves, another person seems like a savior. Pretty soon, however, if they haven't made changes in themselves, they'll feel like a jerk again. And if they're not careful, they'll be blaming their new partner for this feeling—and the cycle continues.

Evolutionary Tip
The Mantras of Pure Divorce

Mantras are useful for quickly reminding yourself of your goals and needs when your Reptilian Brain gets activated by fear or hurt. You'll want your mantras to briefly emphasize what's really important to you, not what you want to have happen to your ex-partner. Here are some examples:

- I need to say good-bye to you and to repair myself.
- I've decided that this relationship is no longer healthy for me.
- I don't want this divorce, but I accept that you no longer want this marriage.
- I need to leave without hurting myself or others.
- By giving up on this relationship, I'm giving up any claims on you, including *all* partnership and sexual rights, except in parenting our children.
- I can no longer influence or change you. I will therefore leave you to your own devices and to God's will.
- I will be as fair to you as I would be to any other human being regarding children, money, and possessions, but I won't let myself be victimized.
- Thoughts of revenge harm me because they keep me in a relationship with you.
- For now, you can no longer help me because we are no longer attached to each other. You don't have the same influence with me you once had.
- I've decided to separate myself from you. Thoughts of you, both negative and positive, are not helpful to me right now. This will remain true until I feel I've fully recovered.

SAYING GOOD-BYE: THE GRIEVING PROCESS

How do you say good-bye to someone who has hurt you deeply, and simultaneously say good-bye to a part of yourself? And how do you deal with the massive overload of emotions and grief, without surrendering to reptilian fight-or-flight responses? The simple answer is that you must allow yourself to grieve. In divorce, you will probably be tempted to focus on what your partner has done to you. This may even be healthy to some degree, as an alternative might be to dwell on your own faults and failures. Taken to extremes, however, either of these pathways will be harmful. If you remain locked in rage at your partner's misdeeds, you'll be unavailable to yourself and to future relationships. If you remain convinced that you're unlovable or unattractive, you won't expect to be loved and admired in other relationships. You may not be sufficiently careful in selecting friends or lovers in the future if you see yourself as damaged goods.

Problem Solving

Let me give you an example of what can go wrong when divorcing couples become reptilian. Many couples become very involved in the "fairness" of visitation arrangements with their children. They agonize and battle over whether each has 50 percent of the time with their children. Sometimes this battle is really about making sure "that I get what is coming to me and that everything, including time with our kids, is split *right down the middle*." This battle is certainly not about the welfare of the children. It's not even about time spent with the children. When they live together, do parents usually have equal time with their kids? Of course not! The most damaging element of this fight is that it often becomes so competitive that the actual needs of both the children and the parents get completely lost. I've seen a number of couples who could have made each other's lives much easier through a flexible and cooperative arrangement of care for the children and who stridently refused to do so due to their ongoing competitive issues.

You can avoid this kind of battle by attempting to separate out what is a practical need of yours and what feels more like a need for revenge or affirmation. This won't be easy, but it is certainly worthwhile. One question you may wish to ask yourself throughout this process is, "What do I really need to have happen at this point? What are my goals or needs? What are my children's needs?" You may have to do some self-soothing (like the Quick Release from Reptilian Responses exercise in Chapter One) in order to slow down and think creatively. Once you've done that, you'll probably find that what you were about to say or do in the heat of the moment was actually least likely to give you the desired results.

Let's say your goal is to have Wednesday nights with your children because that's your short workday, and that would give you more time with them. Earlier we discussed the stories that partners hold regarding each other based on injuries or old rhythms in their relationship. Perhaps you imagine that your partner won't agree to your request for Wednesday nights because "He'll do anything to hurt me" or "She's so anal about this sharing thing that she'll want every other Wednesday." You might then be tempted to go on the attack and tell your partner, "You'd probably just let them sit around drinking sodas and watching TV, while I intend to do something educational with them." Is this likely to make your former partner more cooperative? I don't think so. You may also consider whining, nagging, or tricking your former partner, all of which may seem necessary but will ultimately lead to greater conflict.

As you think about the Wednesday problem, can you see any way to negotiate? If this were a simple time management issue at work, you know you could find a solution to satisfy everyone. You need to separate the history of injuries that led up to the divorce from the current request for time with the children. Your partner may not cooperate, but there may also be ways to encourage him or her to slow down and communicate based on mutual needs, once you stop using competitive and angry language.

Rituals of Grief

As you work through the business of divorce give yourself time and space to grieve. You may need a ritual or celebration to affirm that life goes on after divorce. You may need to read about divorce; there are many excellent books on the subject, a few of which are included in the Resources. It is necessary for you to come to grips with the fact that many of the things that you imagined were going to happen between you and your partner will never happen—and that—at least for a time—you'll be alone. If you believe that this grief process should happen quickly, you may be angry and impatient with yourself for not simply getting over it. Grief takes a different amount of time for each person. Two years isn't unusual for significant recovery. This doesn't mean that you're likely to be in full-blown pain for two years; it means that this isn't an unusual amount of time to really work through the many stages of hurt, confusion, disappointment, anger, and fear that typically arise in divorce.

I warn you of this so that you won't feel bad about yourself if you're still hurting six months after the divorce and, more important, so that you won't move too quickly into another relationship. People who race from a troubled relationship into a new one usually cheat themselves out of the grieving process and the learning curve that normally occurs during that time. The chances that their new relationship will be haunted by the ghosts of the old one are extremely high. They also lose the valuable experience of successfully being alone.

Grieving includes a lot more than just feeling bad about the past. In Chapter Eight, we talked about your understanding what has happened to you as a means of finding closure. This requires a great deal of courage. Even if you imagine your partner to be totally at fault—which is generally a dangerous position to take—you must still evaluate how this thing happened. You may see your partner as evil or sly or violent, and you may be absolutely right. Even if this is so, however, you must still give some thought to what attracted you to an evil, sly, or violent person. Without such an examination, you're in danger of repeating these problems in the future.

Grief includes five commonly accepted stages: (1) denial, (2) anger, (3) bargaining, (4) depression, and (5) acceptance.[2] People process grief in very different ways, but you may recognize some of these stages in your own reactions. As you think about these steps, is it any wonder that recovery takes some time and that you'll be on a roller coaster emotionally? You may even experience a period of feeling okay, immediately followed by severe panic or depression. Grief will also be reawakened by the landmark moments of the divorce process, and you may feel as though you are revisiting each of the stages of grief at each of these events:

1. The decision and announcement that you and your partner are going to divorce

2. Telling the kids

3. Moving out and finding temporary housing

4. Seeing attorneys or mediators

5. Filing for divorce

6. Selling the house

7. Finding a new permanent home

8. Receiving the final decree

9. The first time your kids meet your ex's new partner

10. The first time your kids meet your new partner

And then there is usually a point somewhere along the path toward divorce where you suddenly become deeply aware that the relationship is dead. This is a sad, horrible moment in which you rouse from denial and are fully aware of your loss at the deepest levels. Don't be surprised if you're tempted to scream.

Given the demands on people during this process, it's not too surprising that wounded partners react angrily with each other. Doing so may protect them from the despair of the actual grief process. Anger and self-righteousness certainly feel more powerful than being wounded and fearful. If you need to release the energy of anger, you may wish to do this at the health club or in some other physically healthy way. Maybe you feel intensely like telling your partner off as well, and let her know how much she's hurt you. If this is a goal, then ask yourself the following question: "What do I still need from my former partner to feel okay about myself?" If you can picture anything that she can say or do that will be helpful, perhaps an apology, then ask for it. Otherwise, if you continue to hold on to these angry or vengeful thoughts, you're deciding to remain in a very frustrating process with no hope of satisfaction or closure. And in many cases there will never be an opportunity for any kind of satisfying emotional closure; accepting that there will be no such opportunity may be the closest you come to closure. You will need to bite your tongue and move on.

PROTECTING YOURSELF
AND YOUR CHILDREN

This chapter is about the majority of divorces, in situations where the two partners are basically sound and decent people who have decided to end their relationship. Unfortunately, that's not always the case. And although I preach about the importance of avoiding revenge, I'm not encouraging you to simply lie down and allow yourself to be harmed in the divorce process. A certain amount of anger can be a healthy thing during the healing process of separation and divorce. And you must protect yourself and your children if that becomes necessary. If you have a vindictive or dangerous partner who becomes threatening during the separation process, then you'll need to enlist the help of attorneys and police. This is not an attempt to control or change your partner: you need to defend yourself, your children, your family, and your possessions, just as you would against any other outside threat.

If you're in a dangerous situation, please get help through counseling and other supports. Check out what your community offers for battered spouses. Meet with an attorney and examine what state laws are relevant to your situation and needs.

Protecting the Children

We're always concerned, of course, about the impact of divorce on children. Some suggest that it's worthwhile to stay in a marriage so that children won't have to suffer through the divorce process.[3]

Extended hostility between parents is damaging to children, whether caused by sustained tension in a hostile, angry marriage or by a lengthy, entrenched divorce. If you're staying in a hostile environment or continuing hostilities in a divorce process and beyond, don't think you're doing your children any favors!

What you see as necessary for the child's well-being may be different from what your former partner wants or what a court of law would agree is necessary. If your partner is likely to harm the children in any manner, your decisions may seem clear, although the nuances of the law may still cause difficulties. Not all issues of what will harm the children are crystal clear, either. Suppose your partner likes to keep your nine-year-old up late on Friday nights to watch what you feel are age-inappropriate movies. What if they're horror movies that scare the hell out of your child—but that he insists he wants to watch? The reality may be that he likes being scared and then comforted by his daddy who is there to protect him. Maybe it's his way of coping with the fear he feels about the divorce and wants to know that his dad (or his mom) will be there when he needs protection. Regardless of the reasons behind the routine, you see it as destructive to the child and want to challenge this practice.

During the divorce process, you'll undoubtedly see things happen in your child's life with which you disagree. You need to choose your battles carefully and—here is the real message—there is hope. The less conflict in the postdivorce relationship you have, the greater the chance that you'll actually be able to convince your ex-partner that letting a child watch a scary or violent movie may not be in the best interests of your nine-year-old and that there are more positive ways to help him feel protected.[4]

The ultimate goal of marital therapy is to greatly improve the health of the individuals in the relationship, not necessarily to save the relationship at all costs. The nonreptilian examination of your relationship may allow the option for the relationship to end and for that end to occur in a cooperative and healthy fashion. This will permit both you and your partner to grow and emancipate as confident, recovered individuals.

The concept of pure divorce is intended to provide some relief from the intense or overwhelming feelings, avoid the more destructive aspects of primitive reptilian behavior, and move partners toward ending their relationship without further injury. No one suggests that divorce should be a pleasant or painless experience. The friendliest divorce I've ever seen was not painless. No one can tell you that you should just get back into the game, start dating, and forget the past. Marriage and divorce are momentous changes and need to be given their sacred due. Considering the seriousness of the situation, partners who do decide to go their separate ways would be well advised to try anything possible to soothe themselves and their partner, and move toward a reasonable method of saying good-bye to each other.

Afterword

A Few Words in Closing

I hope you've received some practical and encouraging information from reading this book. I hope you now know that you fight because you're human. You're not stupid, nor are you necessarily evil. When you perceive a threat, you defend yourself or try to get away, as dictated by a primitive part of your brain. As long as you remain in the threatened position, you'll find it difficult to organize your thoughts, remember key issues, empathize with your partner, and look for solutions. The first goal in solving difficult relationship issues is not to find a solution but to comfort and reassure each other, thus lowering your heart rate, slowing your breathing, relaxing your muscles, and enabling your larger, more evolved brain.

When you understand the basic principles of combat, you are able to recognize your and your partner's primitive defenses and allow yourselves to slow things down. At the same time, I encourage you to challenge each other to increase intimacy by taking responsibility for yourself and seeing to your individual wants and needs. It is the paradox of this work that for you to get closer to each other, you need to first gain some appropriate distance. When you feel less responsible for your partner's anxieties, fears, or happiness, the doors are open to a romantic and intimate relationship.

Throughout this book, you've seen how various methods for slowing down an emotionally charged event with your partner allow you to maintain your highest brain functioning and more clearly define the needs and ideas that both of you bring to a difficult discussion or negotiation. You've learned to stop focusing on large, dynamic changes and to enjoy the benefits of steady, small changes in which you can offer positive things to each other.

You've learned to hope for progress but also to accept that the process won't always be smooth and straightforward. Most often, when there are slips there are also opportunities to reexplore your contract with each other and expand on your learning together. It's through such trial-and-error experimentation and occasional catastrophes that you and your partner can develop a strong sense of yourselves and your relationship.

Finally, you've come to realize that work on your relationship is never done. You may need to repeat the steps in this book, look at books in specific areas, or in other ways continue to explore yourself, your partner, and your relationship. You may need to recognize that there will be no change if your partner makes no effort and appears to be happy with the current state. This is seldom the case, but it does occur. Can you make a good life for yourself without such changes or will you actually need to leave? If you decide to leave, perhaps you will be able to do so with your humanity intact and with forgiveness of your partner's human failings.

In any case, I hope you now realize that we humans are complex and fascinating beings who carry within us the capacity for both destructive primitive behavior, the legacy of our reptilian fight-or-flight brains, but also great insight, transcendence, and love. As you work on your relationship, you will be tempted to return to old ways, or you may fear that your partner does not want what you want out of life. But this is the beginning, the first day of your adventure. Make your wishes known for yourself and your partner. I have seen many, many couples make wonderful discoveries with each other once they were able to relax and explore their relationship. I hope you take this journey as well and have marvelous experiences together.

Notes

Please note: Unless publication information is provided in the note, all publications cited have complete reference listings in the Resources.

Chapter One

1. W. B. Cannon formulated the fight-or-flight reaction in his book *Bodily Changes in Pain, Hunger, Fear and Rage: An Account of Recent Researches into the Functions of Emotional Excitement,* 2nd ed. (New York: Appleton-Century-Crofts, 1929). This concept was greatly expanded in the work of Hans Selye, arguably the father of modern stress management theory. Selye detailed the complexities of the fight-or-flight reaction in *The Story of the Adaptation Syndrome* (Montreal: Acta, 1952).

   Daniel Goleman offers a very readable description of the fight-or-flight reaction and the ways in which emotions interfere with human interactions in his book *Emotional Intelligence: Why It Can Matter More Than IQ.* In chap. 5 he describes the "amygdala hijack," in which emotions overwhelm all normal reasoning abilities.

2. Selye, H. *The Stress of Life.* New York: McGraw-Hill, 1956.

3. Joseph LeDoux has accomplished pioneering work in outlining the role of emotions and cognitive functioning. In *The Emotional Brain: The Mysterious Underpinnings of Emotional Life,* he summarizes the regions of the brain affected by stress, fear, and other emotional

stimuli, and details the effects of these on thinking, memory, decision making, and other cognitive output.

Additionally you may want to read the work of the noted neurologist Dr. Antonio Damasio. He has explained the interrelationships between cognitive functioning, including the ability to reason effectively, and specific regions of the brain. Please see his books *Descartes' Error* (New York: Putnam, 1994) and *The Feeling of What Happens: Body and Emotion in the Making of Consciousness* (New York: Harcourt, 1999).

I must say, however, that if you're inspired to read further at this juncture, I would hope that you would invest most of your reading time in your relationship. Therefore, I refer you to the books in the Resources by John Gottman and Harville Hendrix, who do a wonderful job of relating physical, cognitive, and emotional issues to relationship work.

4. LeDoux describes the instantaneous response to danger that the brain undergoes. The immediacy of this interpretation is such that you can recognize that something is dangerous without realizing how you know. This response is outlined in *The Emotional Brain*.

5. Paul MacLean first described the three levels of brain development in the 1950s. See *The Triune Brain in Evolution: Role in Paleocerebral Functions* (New York: Plenum, 1990) for a summary of his work.

6. You can find detailed descriptions of the role of the Reptilian Brain in communication in Dr. Philip Lieberman's *Human Language and Our Reptilian Brain: The Subcortical Bases of Speech, Syntax, and Thought*. This reference focuses on the neurophysiology of language, however, and does not address relationship issues. It is clear that what we think of as a higher-order phenomenon, human communication, is actually strongly influenced and driven by the Reptilian Brain.

7. Abraham Maslow has theorized that there is a hierarchy of human needs that must be met in a specific order: (1) basic physiological needs; (2) the need for safety; (3) the needs for belonging and love; (4) the need for self-esteem; and (5) what Maslow described as the need for self-actualization. Looking at this hierarchy, one notes

that the need to feel safe precedes most other considerations; if you don't feel safe, you won't be able to access higher abilities that allow you to achieve affiliation, love, self-esteem, and self-actualization. See Maslow's *Motivation and Personality*, 2nd ed. (New York: HarperCollins, 1970).

Chapter Two

1. In his book *After the Fight: Using Your Disagreements to Build a Stronger Relationship*, Daniel Wile describes this behavior simply as "developing symptoms." In his view, partners' experience of scary, sad, or angry feelings and the resulting attack or escape are simply a symptom of their pain, which can be treated and altered.

2. I again refer you to Paul MacLean's groundbreaking work, which demonstrated the role of the primitive limbic brain in the responses of a person who feels threatened: MacLean, P. "The Limbic Systems with Respect to Self-Preservation and the Preservation of the Species." *Journal of Nervous and Mental Disorders*, 1958, *127*, 1–11.

3. In *After the Honeymoon: How Conflict Can Improve Your Relationship*, Daniel Wile describes marital conflict as being about the conversation the couple never had but needed to have. He describes the need to use the conflict or disagreement in the relationship to develop intimacy, and notes how the avoidance of the tough discussions leads to gradual distancing of partners from one another.

4. I can't overstate the importance of the ability to return to difficult subjects and press for intimacy through the conflict. Such persistence is difficult and risky, and it's absolutely normal that we try to avoid such uncomfortable discussions. But in deepening the relationship, as described by Wile (in *After the Fight* and *After the Honeymoon*), and in preventing betrayal (see Shirley Glass's *Not "Just Friends"*), we recognize the advantages of courageously approaching these topics when the Reptilian Brain has been quieted.

5. I have not discussed stalking, which is perhaps the ultimate act of pathological control and well beyond the bounds of this book. For more information, see the following: Davis, K. E., Frieze, I. H., and

Maiuro, R. D. *Stalking: Perspectives on Victims and Perpetrators*. New York: Springer, 2002.

Chapter Three

1. It's often said that the best defense is a good offense. Well, it's also the most natural. In his Nobel Prize–winning masterpiece, *Crowds and Power* (New York: Continuum, 1973), Elias Canetti details the ways in which the primitive imperative is to defeat a perceived enemy, no matter what cost.

2. Daniel Wile *(After the Honeymoon)* describes changing your view of your partner by carefully reassessing your own interpretations. In other words, your relationship might change simply by virtue of your thinking about your partner's behaviors from a new perspective.

3. Social psychology teaches us that we are influenced at a profound level by those around us. If you answer the self-assessment items together with your partner, you'll be tempted to respond in a way that either makes your answers palatable to him or her or gets a reaction. The first round of responses should be about you and for you.

4. It is well documented that stress causes sleep problems, changes in appetite, muscle tension, and decreased efficiency of the immune system, as suggested in Hans Selye's *The Stress of Life* (New York: McGraw-Hill, 1956). Stress can cause marital difficulties, and marital difficulties are stressful. You must disrupt this cycle by treating as many of the contributing factors as possible, including decreasing your negative physical responses to stress and increasing your healthy responses, while also working on your relationship. Please see the references under Stress Management in the Resources.

5. Symptoms of depression, anxiety, or panic can include insomnia, changes in appetite, difficulties with concentration and memory, increased suspiciousness, muscle tension, headaches, gastric problems, irritability, anger outbursts, and confusion. Some relationship problems can be related to or causing such symptoms in one or both partners.

6. See Stress Management in the Resources for additional aids.

7. Some will assume that a decreased interest in sex is due to a loss of interest in their partner, to their age, or to some other dangerous and likely permanent condition. In shame, a person may even try to pretend that it's not an issue. Bernie Zilbergeld describes numerous possible reasons for changes in sexual desire in *The New Male Sexuality: The Truth About Men, Sex, and Pleasure*. Many are amazed at how treatable such conditions can be when properly evaluated. See the Sexuality section in the Resources for more help.

8. Many people don't realize that the natural propensity of the body in times of stress, and particularly with extended periods of insomnia, is to go on full alert, which can take the form of suspiciousness bordering on paranoia.

9. Has anger intruded in other areas of your life as well as in your marriage? Do you need to examine your anger as an individual issue and get that under control, as part of the work on your relationship? See the Anger section in the Resources for some excellent references.

10. Harville Hendrix (*Getting the Love You Want*) masterfully describes the role of family history in mate selection as well as in relationship development and conflict.

11. The term *psychological contract* has primarily been used in business management literature since the 1960s. This term summarizes the development of the expectations in intimate relationships as well. For more information, see the following resources: Robinson, S. L., and Rousseau, D. M. "Violating the Psychological Contract: Not the Exception but the Norm." *Journal of Behavior*, Nov. 7, 1994, pp. 245–259; Schermerhorn, J. R., Jr. *Management*. (7th ed.) New York: Wiley, 2002.

12. The concept of "stories" has been described in books for clinicians doing marital and family therapy. For more information, see the following: White, M., and Epstein, D. *Narrative Means to Therapeutic Ends*. New York: Norton, 1990; O'Hanlon Hudson, P., and Hudson O'Hanlon, W. *Rewriting Love Stories: Brief Marital Therapy*. New York: Norton, 1991.

Chapter Four

1. Remember that even couples who feel they are ignoring each other are actually hyperaware and watchful of each other. This awareness does not facilitate intimacy. Rather it drives partners further away from each other and behind their barricades. The primitive need to defend territory, particularly when threatened, is well known in science. In *The Territorial Imperative* (New York: Atheneum, 1966), Robert Ardrey describes this drive among animals, humans, and groups. The more threatened you feel, the more you'll want to pull into yourself and protect your boundaries. You may watch your partner warily, anticipating and fearing any kind of intrusion. You might then interpret even a mild intrusion, such as a question, as an assault requiring flight or counterattack.

2. Just for fun, rent the movie *The Ref* (Touchstone Pictures, 1994). Early in the film there's a scene between Judy Davis and Kevin Spacey with their marital therapist, in which they try to score points off of each other. It's a very funny, very sad scene that nicely captures the cognitive confusion of reptilian battle.

3. In treating anxious people, I often ask them to organize their thoughts and concerns by writing them down. Just the act of writing uses more of the brain. Forcing your thoughts onto paper also cuts down on wheel-spinning, repetitive thinking. It helps you feel more in control, at least of your own thoughts. You can also use the brief time it takes to write down a note to gather your thoughts.

4. A heightened startle response to sudden noises, movement, or touch is often seen in persons with anxiety or posttraumatic stress disorder. For more information, see the following: van der Kolk, B. A. "The Body Keeps the Score: Approaches to the Psychobiology of Posttraumatic Stress Disorder." In B. A. van der Kolk, A. C. McFarlane, and L. Weisaeth (eds.), *Traumatic Stress: The Effects of Overwhelming Experience on Mind, Body, and Society*. New York: Guilford Press, 1996.

Chapter Five

1. In *The Emotional Brain* (pp. 163–166), Joseph LeDoux describes
reception and interpretation of a threatening sound by way of primitive pathways to the amygdala versus more advanced pathways
(thalamus receptors to the neocortex). The amygdala pathways are
less refined and specific but almost instantaneous in their response
to a threat. The cortical pathways more accurately define the source
and nature of the sound, but it takes more time and delays the
response. This is a small, specific example of the separation in the
brain of unconscious, emotionally driven responses and conscious
ones. When threatened, the brain does a poorer job of organizing
data and problem solving because the pathways for immediately preventing harm are dominating the response.

2. Daniel Goleman's *Emotional Intelligence* (pp. 13–29) provides an
excellent description of the process by which we rapidly prepare for
self-defense when expecting a threat or misinterpreting an event as
a threat. In human interaction, the protective response will be seen
as threatening by the partner.

3. Frank Pittman (*Private Lies*) and Shirley Glass (*Not "Just Friends"*)
present strong cases for flirting as a dangerous display of availability
by a partner. Even if not intended as a serious offer of an affair, flirting opens the door.

4. Please refer to the Money section in the Resources for books specifically
related to the role money plays in relationship issues. These provide
numerous examples of the symbolic importance of money in your life.

5. Cloé Madanes describes the symbolic meaning of money in *The
Secret Meaning of Money: How It Binds Together Families in Love,
Envy, Compassion or Anger* (San Francisco: Jossey-Bass, 1994).

6. Victoria F. Collins (*Couples and Money*) and Mary Claire Allvine
and Christine Larson (*The Family CFO*) provide forms and outlines
for structuring your expenses and financial goals.

7. In *After the Fight* (pp. 75–76), Daniel Wile discusses the advantages
and disadvantages of interrupting and provides rules for how to

interrupt most effectively when it's necessary. I encourage you to use great caution in interrupting, as it tends to throw off and shut down the speaker. If your partner fears that by interrupting you're signaling that you won't listen, then she will have to intensify her message. It's a short step from here to a reptilian episode.

8. Franks, M. *How to Get Your Point Across in 30 Seconds or Less*. New York: Pocket Books, 1986.

Chapter Six

1. Michelle Weiner Davis has discussed such relationships and their treatment in her book *The Sex-Starved Marriage*. I would also suggest David Schnarch's book *Resurrecting Sex*.

2. In *The Seven Principles for Making Marriage Work* (pp. 83–86), John Gottman and Nan Silver describe exercises for consciously adding positives into your relationship. This "emotional bank account" is the repository of positive feelings about each other and reminders that you are each other's best support. Disappointments or minor disagreements hold little power against a well-stocked account.

Chapter Seven

1. In *The Sex-Starved Marriage*, Michele Weiner Davis describes the various causes for a loss of sexual intimacy, not just in elderly couples but across the life span.

2. Every man and perhaps every woman as well should read Bernie Zilbergeld's book *The New Male Sexuality*. Zilbergeld masterfully details the origin of many harmful myths about sex, which place incredible barriers in the pathway to relaxing, comforting, and exciting sexual intimacy.

3. You may be a little shy about selecting a book on sex if you've never done so before. Forget about it! I'm forever taking out stacks of books on sexuality at my local bookstore and library, and no one raises an eyebrow. Many of these books, such as Alex Comfort's *The Joy of Sex*, are tastefully presented and will help you learn about yourself and your partner and develop your intimate relationship in a safe manner.

Chapter Eight

1. Sexual misbehavior comes in many forms and this particular case is one of sexual addiction. Frank Pittman has described various types of infidelity and the resulting traumas and needs in *Private Lies*.

2. Patrick Carnes has written extensively on sexual addictions and Internet pornography addiction. For more information on these topics, you can refer to the following: Carnes, P. *Out of the Shadows: Understanding Sexual Addiction*. (2nd ed.) Center City, Minn.: Hazeldon, 1992; Carnes, P., Delmonico, D., and Griffin, E. *In the Shadows of the Net: Breaking Free of Compulsive Online Sexual Behavior*. Center City, Minn.: Hazeldon, 2001.

3. In *Not "Just Friends,"* Shirley Glass describes the essence of flirting and emotional connections to an attractive person other than your partner. Many people assert that they enjoy engaging in "harmless flirting." They say, "Hey, it's just my style. I don't mean anything by it, and my wife knows it's not serious." Maybe this is even true sometimes. Flirting, however, also functions as a signal that you are available (p. 41). Broadcasting that you are likely open to infidelity conflicts with your marital intimacy. If your offer is always out there, eventually someone is likely to take you up on it.

4. Shirley Glass has eloquently described the slippery slope that many find themselves on when they are developing a relationship with a person who is more than "just a good friend." She explains the three "red flags" indicating that a platonic relationship is becoming something more: (1) emotional intimacy, (2) secrecy, and (3) sexual chemistry.

   In *Emotional Infidelity*, M. Gary Neuman clarifies that sexual intercourse is not necessary in order for an extramarital relationship to create a wound in the marital relationship.

5. For more discussion of this topic, please see Susan Forward's *Toxic In-Laws*. Respecting family ties while protecting your marriage can require very delicate maneuvering.

6. Many of the partners in such couples have adopted rather inflexible roles. One is the patient-invalid and the other may be the long-suffering, loving-but-angry, and nagging caretaker. When the drinking stops, both roles dramatically change. The caretaker is expected to

go into a kind of semiretirement from a position in which he or she is skilled. You may wish to look at the literature on codependency or other references on living with an addict for more information.

7. See Fred Luskin's book *Forgive for Good*.

8. You may not recognize the title of this poem, but if you've seen *Four Weddings and a Funeral*, you undoubtedly remember its being spoken for a deceased partner, in a truly moving scene.

Chapter Nine

1. Research on therapist efficacy is reviewed in the following: Lambert, M. J., and Bergin, A. E. "Effectiveness in Psychotherapy." In A. E. Bergin and S. Garfield (eds.), *Handbook of Psychotherapy and Behavior Change*. (4th ed.) New York: Wiley, 1994.

2. I have a confession to make. Although I am a trained psychologist, know this material intimately, and teach it repeatedly throughout my week, I have still been known to react in reptilian fashion when taken unawares or sufficiently threatened or hurt. Because the reptilian response uses a different part of our brains, we need to practice easily available methods for stemming the process early and helping our partners do the same.

Chapter Ten

1. Such a positive approach to divorce is also discussed in Constance Ahrons's *The Good Divorce*, Mel and Pat Krantzler's *The New Creative Divorce*, and Craig and Sandra Volgy Everett's *Healthy Divorce*.

2. Kübler-Ross, E. *On Death and Dying*. Old Tappan, N.J.: Macmillan, 1969.

3. In *The Unexpected Legacy of Divorce*, Judith Wallerstein and her colleagues have demonstrated the negative effects divorce has on children and that these effects extend into adulthood. Also see Michelle Weiner Davis's *Divorce Busting*.

4. There are many fine books on helping children through divorce. For example, M. Gary Neuman uses a structured approach in *Helping Your Kids Cope with Divorce the Sandcastles Way*.

Resources

There is a great wealth of references on marriage, relationships, sex, and divorce. I'm sure that I am grievously insulting some excellent authors by not mentioning them here. This list is an attempt to provide a smattering of references in specific areas mentioned throughout the book.

Anger

Lerner, Harriet. *The Dance of Anger: A Woman's Guide to Changing the Patterns of Intimate Relationships*. New York: HarperCollins, 1985. This book was a best-seller for good reason. Many of my clients have identified closely with the patterns described by the author and have found help in this book. A strong focus on family history gives a sense of pattern and culture to complicated and surprising behaviors. The author explores the difficulties women experience in managing and expressing anger successfully.

McKay, Matthew, Peter Rogers, and Judith McKay. *When Anger Hurts: Quieting the Storm Within*. Oakland, Calif.: New Harbinger, 1989. This is a book I regularly recommend and have used as a guide for my anger management groups. It clearly describes anger management techniques in a step-by-step approach that will appeal to many people who don't think of themselves as having an anger problem, as well as to those who have already identified their difficulties with anger.

Tavris, Carol. *Anger: The Misunderstood Emotion*. New York: Touchstone, 1989. The author provides a well-researched evaluation of this emotion, with a focus on the positive uses of anger as well as its more harmful effects. She reviews types of anger and explores common myths about this complex human response.

Betrayal

Glass, Shirley. Not "Just Friends": Rebuilding Trust and Recovering Your Sanity After Infidelity. New York: Free Press, 2003. This is really an extremely helpful book. The author has combined research and clinical experience to demonstrate the many ways in which people, even those in good marriages, become embroiled in affairs. She clarifies that many relationships, which initially appear to be between "just good friends," are actually drifting toward a romantic attachment. Such friendships become increasingly secretive and special and exclude the partner. Glass describes an approach to protecting the marital relationship and recovering when betrayal has occurred.

Luskin, Fred. Forgive for Good: A Proven Prescription for Health and Happiness. New York: HarperCollins, 2002. Surviving betrayal requires the ability to forgive yourself and your partner. Luskin offers a plan for mastering this skill. Injured partners often struggle with questions of forgiveness and whether they are being true to themselves if they strive to forgive their lover. Luskin provides ways of exploring such questions and growing as a healthy individual.

Neuman, M. Gary. Emotional Infidelity. New York: Crown, 2001. Every person who feels that she can become intimately close to a coworker or friend without harming her primary relationship should read this book. Neuman challenges the idea that if there is no sex, then there is no foul, and offers proposals for improving and ensuring the safety of the primary relationship.

Pittman, Frank. Private Lies: Infidelity and the Betrayal of Intimacy. New York: Norton, 1989. This is a fascinating and comprehensive exploration of betrayal in intimate relationships. Pittman examines the wide span of beliefs about and reasons for affairs, and provides guidance for recovery in the primary relationship. He explains four kinds of affairs, and anyone who has been involved in or injured by infidelity will recognize himself or herself in this book.

Couples Communication

Gottman, John, and Nan Silver. The Seven Principles for Making Marriage Work. New York: Crown, 1999. I haven't listed a lot of general marital communication books because there are just too many of them, but this is one that I've found to be most useful. Gottman is a recognized expert in the field, and his work is grounded in careful follow-up research. He and Silver describe marriages that work and those that don't, with a careful eye to practical and workable solutions. The exercises and experiments they propose are tested and proven to be helpful.

Gray, John. *Men Are from Mars, Women Are from Venus*. New York: HarperCollins, 1992. The author describes in a helpful manner clear differences in the way men and women approach communication, togetherness, and intimacy, and describes clearly why they may misinterpret each other's motives. I don't focus much on gender differences in my work, but many have found considerable relief in recognizing their own behaviors in Gray's descriptions.

Hendrix, Harville. *Getting the Love You Want: A Guide for Couples*. New York: HarperCollins, 1998. This is an outstanding book. Hendrix offers a thorough and insightful examination of primitive brain functioning and how this affects our choices and behaviors in developing love relationships. He also delves into the impact of family culture on the relationship. He provides a sound and practical process for exploring and developing as individuals and partners.

Lerner, Harriet. *The Dance of Connection*. New York: HarperCollins, 2001. This is an excellent description of effective communication techniques with persons who have injured you or who are for some other reason difficult for you to deal with. The book goes far beyond couples issues into a variety of relationship puzzles.

Markman, Howard J., Scott M. Stanley, and Susan L. Blumberg. *Fighting for Your Marriage: Positive Steps for Preventing Divorce and Preserving a Lasting Love* (New and Revised). San Francisco: Jossey-Bass, 2001. The authors have based their assessment and approach on years of careful research, and they present a clear rationale for their interventions. This is another of those books that I would use as a next step in your work together. The authors' steps to building a strong relationship are practical and completely doable.

Waite, Linda, and Maggie Gallagher. *The Case for Marriage*. New York: Broadway Books, 2000. This is an excellent review of literature, research, and surveys demonstrating the advantages of the marital relationship for both men and women in all areas of human functioning. Statistically, married people are healthier and happier, have better sex, and are financially better off—not to mention the obvious advantages for children. Of course, we need to work to make marriages rewarding and joyous.

Weiner-Davis, Michelle. *Divorce Busting*. New York: Summit Books, 1992. The author presents a strong case for staying together if at all possible. Early in the book, she proposes that "divorce is not the answer" and prescribes practical ways of rebuilding the relationship.

Wile, Daniel. *After the Honeymoon: How Conflict Can Improve Your Relationship*. New York: Wiley, 1988. Wile is one of those writers whom couples therapists and seminar presenters always seem to be quoting. This book demonstrates how couples benefit from working through conflict and how successful conflict resolution builds intimacy. He points out that most marital battles and estrangements are related to the argument couples should have had but didn't. The partners' real issues may be hidden from each other and even from themselves, and therefore work behind the scenes to keep the couple apart.

_____. *After the Fight: Using Your Disagreements to Build a Stronger Relationship*. New York: Guilford Press, 1993. Wile examines a night in the life of a troubled couple and uses this one series of disagreements as a means of explaining the complexities of intimate battle. In this approach, he shows how the overt discussion doesn't really give much insight into the true needs and fears of the partners. He then demonstrates how they can pull themselves out of this spiral and work together to build their relationship. Above all, he shows how dangerous it is for partners to avoid the true issues between them.

Divorce

Ahrons, Constance. *The Good Divorce: Keeping Your Family Together When Your Marriage Comes Apart*. New York: HarperCollins, 1995. If you must consider divorce, then it's wise to do so with as much information in hand as possible. The less you are taken by surprise, the less intense will be your pain and anger, and the fewer horrible errors you will make. This is an excellent reference that covers a wide range of issues inherent in ending a relationship.

Everett, Craig, and Sandra Volgy Everett. *Healthy Divorce*. San Francisco: Jossey-Bass, 1994. The Everetts offer a brief and useful overview of the fourteen stages of divorce. They provide insights helpful for smoothing the most difficult steps in ending a marriage. Their approach is very relevant to what I have described in this book as pure divorce.

Krantzler, Mel, and Pat Krantzler. *The New Creative Divorce: How to Create a Happier, More Rewarding Life During—and After—Your Divorce*. Holbrook, Mass.: Adams Media, 1998. A very readable self-help guide for making divorce less devastating. The authors encourage couples to focus on living after divorce and what will allow them to get past the rage and self-destructive actions that too often occur. This book also provides realistic approaches to maintaining connection with children and guarding their safety in a divorce.

Neuman, M. Gary. *Helping Your Kids Cope with Divorce the Sandcastles Way*. New York: Random House, 1998. Neuman guides parents in cushioning their children's experience throughout the divorce process. He uses a common-sense approach, broken down by age so that his interventions are targeted and age appropriate. He also describes the various stages of divorce and recovery through the child's perspective. The exercises he provides can be fun and informative and increase the safety and intimacy of your child's relationship with both of you.

Vaughan, Diane. *Uncoupling: Turning Points in Intimate Relationships*. New York: Oxford University Press, 1986. Ending a relationship is generally painful and confusing. Vaughan has provided one of the most useful roadmaps available. This book remains an important and accessible guide for staying healthy during the ending of a relationship.

Wallerstein, Judith, Julia Lewis, and Sandra Blakeslee. *The Unexpected Legacy of Divorce: The 25 Year Landmark Study*. New York: Hyperion, 2000. On the basis of their studies, Wallerstein and her colleagues assert that children of divorced parents experience greater difficulties than similar children from intact families. Problems include lower grades and higher rates of substance abuse as well as higher risk for other mental health problems. The "unexpected" aspect of the study was how reliably these effects extended into adulthood for most of the people studied.

Family-of-Origin Issues

Forward, Susan. *Toxic In-Laws: Loving Strategies for Protecting Your Marriage*. New York: HarperCollins, 2001. For many couples, negotiating the balancing act of respecting their parents and protecting their marriage will be the most perilous challenge they will face. Forward offers a comprehensive and thoughtful discussion of these issues. She proposes rational and loving approaches to the challenge of difficult in-law relationships. (When I purchased this book, the sales clerk looked at me with compassion and said, "Good luck." Apparently she could relate to the title.)

Fight-or-Flight Response

Please note: In *Reptiles in Love* I have described a very simplified version of extraordinarily complex physical events. My apologies to the brilliant scientists and authors cited here and to any I have missed who have provided detailed descriptions of neurological processes that boggle most of our minds. Some of these books are not easy reads, but if you are interested in further understanding the brain and the fight-or-flight response, these are important references. If you have not previously studied in this area, you may wish to begin with Goleman's *Emotional Intelligence*.

Damasio, Antonio. *Descartes' Error: Emotion, Reason, and the Human Brain*. New York: Putnam, 1994. This is a fairly complex look at forms of selective damage to the brain and the changes these bring about in personality and functions. The descriptions in chaps. 4 and 7 particularly highlight the impact of the limbic system on emotional and rational functions.

Goleman, Daniel. *Emotional Intelligence: Why It Can Matter More Than IQ*. New York: Bantam Books, 1995.

_____. *Working with Emotional Intelligence*. New York: Bantam Books, 1998. With these two books, Goleman has rendered a great service to the understanding of emotional intelligence and its role in decision making, relationships, and managing one's life in general. The overview in the original book, *Emotional Intelligence*, is excellent and gives more extensive descriptions of some of the brain processes that I have only briefly illustrated. See chap. 2, "Anatomy of an Emotional Hijacking," for a summary of this response as well as a summary of the work of neuroscientist Joseph LeDoux. In *Working with Emotional Intelligence*, Goleman applies these principles to business and management issues.

LeDoux, Joseph. *The Emotional Brain: The Mysterious Underpinnings of Emotional Life*. New York: Simon & Schuster, 1998. LeDoux has accomplished groundbreaking work in linking emotions and our reasoning abilities to specific brain functions. He is quoted in every publication of value in this field. There is a summary of some of his salient points in Goleman's *Emotional Intelligence*.

Lieberman, Philip. *Human Language and Our Reptilian Brain: The Subcortical Bases of Speech, Syntax, and Thought*. Cambridge, Mass.: Harvard University Press, 2000. This is a very detailed reference demonstrating specific areas of the Reptilian Brain that affect communication skills. Lieberman describes ways in which basic communication is not much different for humans and animals. I have mentioned our ability to continue talking and fighting when higher-level thinking is unavailable to us, and have asked you to take this on faith and as represented by your own experience. Lieberman explains the science behind this perplexing state of affairs.

Midlife Couples

Brody, Steve, and Cathy Brody. *Renew Your Marriage at Midlife*. New York: Perigee, 1999. This guide offers useful focus on reestablishing and developing attachment at the midpoint of the relationship. With all the hype about midlife crisis, the challenge to use midlife tensions toward positive development and growth is welcome. This book is well written and accessible and full of excellent tips and exercises; couples with some time together would be well advised to explore it.

Money

Allvine, Mary, and Christine Larson. *The Family CFO: The Couple's Business Plan for Love and Money*. Emmaus, Penn.: Rodale, 2004. I particularly like this book's approach to comparing family financial issues to a business plan. It's an apt comparison that I use frequently in treatment with couples. Partners need to separate the personal issues of power, autonomy, and respect from the business of actual financial needs and concerns. This book will be helpful in outlining those needs.

Collins, Victoria F. *Couples and Money: A Couples' Guide Updated for the New Millennium*. Sherman Oaks, Calif.: Gabriel, 1998. The author explores the role money plays in relationships and how money relates to issues of power, individuation, self-control, respect, and sex. A good step-by-step guide for couples trying to develop a more respectful negotiation about financial issues.

Mellan, Olivia. *Money Harmony: Resolving Money Conflicts in Your Life and Relationships*. New York: Walker, 1994. A basic premise of this book is that in terms of approaches to money management, opposites seem to attract. That is, if one partner tends to save, the other will spend, and if there are other difficulties in the relationship, the financial conflict will be highlighted as a way in which partners make each other uncomfortable. Mellan offers strategies for de-emphasizing these differences and negotiating practical partnership goals.

Parenting

Borba, Michele. *Parents Do Make a Difference: How to Raise Kids with Solid Character, Strong Minds, and Caring Hearts*. San Francisco: Jossey-Bass, 1999. Borba offers eight "success skills" for enhancing your child's development as a whole person. Her approach involves you working with your child to fully realize his or her potential and develop a sense of caring about others.

Phelan, Thomas W. *1-2-3 Magic: Effective Discipline for Children 2–12*. Glen
Ellyn, Ill.: Child Management, 1995. Having heard Thomas Phelan
speak, and having much appreciated this book, I find his approach to be
the most pragmatic and humane of parenting approaches. He promotes
respect of both the parent and the child and removes the aggression and
intensity from the parenting role. By the way, he is a wonderful presenter;
I would recommend that you try either to see him in person or to obtain
his video of the same title as this book.

Sexuality

Comfort, Alex. *The Joy of Sex: Fully Revised and Completely Updated for the 21st
Century*. New York: Crown, 2002. This classic sexual guide provides in-
depth but easily understood descriptions of sexual issues, with a common-
sense approach to healthy sexuality that is refreshing. *The Joy of Sex* offers
ideas for expanding sexual experience while also describing health and
safety issues.

Love, Patricia, and Jo Robinson. *Hot Monogamy: Essential Steps to More Passionate, Intimate Lovemaking*. New York: Plume, 1995. This is a very handy
book. Sexual concerns are described clearly and with compassion. The
authors provide brief assessment tools that will really help you clarify
what you want from each other and what might be getting in the way.
They also use many quotes from participants in their work, which makes
this work feel more personal and relevant.

Schnarch, David. *Passionate Marriage: Sex, Love, and Intimacy in Emotionally
Committed Relationships*. New York: Norton, 1997. Schnarch is widely
known among marital and sex therapists for his pioneering development
of the "sexual crucible" approach to sexual difficulties. This book and the
next are written for couples. In *Passionate Marriage*, Schnarch lays out a
clear description of his methods, which do not rely on sexual techniques
but rather focus on the overall relationship of the couple and their individual abilities to give and receive stimulation. As an important part of
this exchange of stimulation and pleasure he emphasizes their ability to
individuate from one another and therefore develop greater intimacy.
This idea sounds counterintuitive, which is exactly why you may want to
read his book.

_____. *Resurrecting Sex: Resolving Sexual Problems and Rejuvenating Your Rela-
tionship*. New York: HarperCollins, 2002. I particularly like Schnarch's
work because he also emphasizes the role of the Reptilian Brain in relationships and in sexual functioning. Here he describes the myths and fears

that lead to sexual dysfunction. He describes the sexual experience as being measured by "total stimulation." Couples often mistake the physical aspects of arousal and sexual response with their feelings for each other, yet these are two separate factors. This book is shorter than *Passionate Marriage* and combines Schnarch's work from that book and his earlier book for therapists, *Constructing the Sexual Crucible*.

Weiner Davis, Michele. *The Sex-Starved Marriage: A Couple's Guide to Boosting Their Marriage Libido*. New York: Simon & Schuster, 2003. This is a little lighter reading than the books of David Schnarch, but Weiner provides a good description of failure of intimacy in a wide variety of circumstances. Couples will certainly recognize themselves in this book. It provides practical steps toward reintroducing sexual enjoyment into your relationship.

Westheimer, Ruth. *Encyclopedia of Sex*. Jerusalem: Jerusalem Publishing House, 1994. Sometimes it's useful to have a quick reference for sexual terms or concepts, particularly those that you think you should already know. This reference explains and defines terminology, history, practices, and legal issues related to sexuality.

Zilbergeld, Bernie. *The New Male Sexuality: The Truth About Men, Sex, and Pleasure*. New York: Bantam, 1999. This may be the most frequently recommended book for men experiencing relationship or sexual problems. Women may also want to read this, however, as they explore their partner's needs, fears, and motivations. This is a treasure chest of information about male sexuality and the myths that often confound men's attempts at intimacy.

Stress Management

Davis, Martha, Elizabeth Eshelman, and Matthew McKay. *The Relaxation and Stress Reduction Workbook*. (5th ed.) Oakland, Calif.: New Harbinger, 2000. This is a comprehensive and easy–to-follow guide to a wealth of relaxation techniques. The success of specific relaxation techniques tends to be highly individual, so a guide such as this that walks you through numerous options is worth its weight in gold.

Goudey, Pat. *The Unofficial Guide to Beating Stress*. Foster City, Calif.: IDG Books Worldwide, 2000. This is another useful guide that provides information about the causes of stress, the effects of poorly managed stress, and stress management techniques.

Kabat-Zinn, Jon. *Full Catastrophe Living: Using the Wisdom of Your Body and Mind to Face Stress, Pain, and Illness*. New York: Dell, 1990. This is a wonderful overview of meditation and stress reduction techniques. Kabat-Zinn reviews the body's complex stress responses and provides targeted methods of stress reduction as well as mental and physical healing.

_____. *Wherever You Go, There You Are: Mindfulness Meditation in Everyday Life*. New York: Hyperion, 1994. This book offers specific descriptions of various forms of mindfulness meditations and easy-to-follow descriptions of how to achieve meditative states.

———

Here are the addresses and Web sites of a few of the national organizations that can provide you with lists of therapists. Remember, many of these organizations will have state subdivisions that might have more information for your specific area.

American Association of Marriage and Family Therapists
112 South Alfred Street
Alexandria, VA 22314
Phone: (703) 838-9808
Fax: (703) 838-9805
www.aamft.org

National Register of Health Service Providers
1120 G Street NW, Suite 330
Washington, DC 20005
Phone: (202) 783-7663
Fax: (202) 347-0550
www.nationalregister.org

American Psychological Association
750 First Street NE
Washington, DC 20002
Phone: (202) 336-5500; toll free: (800) 374-2721
www.apa.org

National Association of Social Workers
750 First Street NE, Suite 700
Washington, DC 20002
Phone: (202) 408-8600
www.naswdc.org

American Association of Sex Educators,
Counselors and Therapists
P.O. Box 1960
Ashland, VA 23005
Phone: (804) 752-0026
Fax: (804) 752-0026
www.aasect.org

Group therapy may be the most effective intervention for couples. Look for couples groups being offered in your area. If you have difficulty locating such opportunities, you might contact any of your local public mental health centers or any group psychotherapy practice in your area or contact the American Group Psychotherapy Association.

American Group Psychotherapy Association
25 East 21st Street, 6th floor
New York, NY 10010
Phone: (212) 477-2677; toll free: (877) 668-2472
Fax: (212) 979-6627
www.agpa.org
e-mail: info@agpa.org

About the Author

Don Ferguson, Ph.D., is a licensed psychologist; he received his doctoral degree from the University of Kansas. He is a member of the American Association of Marriage and Family Therapists, the American Group Psychotherapy Association, and the American Psychological Association, and is listed with the National Register of Health Service Providers. He has worked as both a therapist and a clinical administrator, the combination of which furthered his understanding of interpersonal relationships. He is a therapist first and foremost, however, having spent more than twenty-five years working with a wide variety of people presenting with all kinds of problems, and often being sought out by couples who have struggled in other forms of treatment. His busy clinical practice in Madison, Wisconsin, includes couples, groups, and individuals. His workshops for couples and his training seminars for therapists, which he conducts throughout the United States and Canada, have received high praise for his practical approach, comfort with the subject, and humor. He has also presented extensively for a wide range of public and private organizations. His presentations on work relationships bring the concept of negative physiological arousal and the resulting loss of intellectual clarity to work groups and administrators.

In order to create a dialogue around relationship issues, Don would very much like to receive any comments or questions you may have about this book. Please see his Web sites at www.reptilesinlove. com or www.donfergusonseminars.com.

Index

W